Loving **Jesus**

Jeff

Delight in the Lord

Whose Joy is Our Strength

Mark Allan Powell

# CONTENTS

This book arose out of conversations that I have had with a number of people over the years regarding my spiritual journey (thus far). Those who have helped me to understand my experiences in light of Scripture, sound reason, and the experiences of others are probably too numerous to mention. I do wish, however, to name a handful of persons who provided direct feedback on the manuscript for this book. I sent the first draft to individuals whom I regard as spiritual role models in one way or another: Walter Bouman, Clayton Croy, Loxi Dailey, David Mann, Scot McKnight, Erick Nelson, Melissa Curtis Powell, Joy Schroeder, and Han van den Blink. All of these people offered advice and comments. They should not be blamed for peculiarities that remain (I did not *always* heed their warnings), but they can be credited with a number of significant improvements that will make the book more rewarding for you than it would have been otherwise. Join me in thanking them. Let us also extend our appreciation to Trinity Lutheran Seminary for granting me the time, support, and encouragement necessary to complete this book, and to Fortress Press (especially editors James Korsmo, Michael West, and Scott Tunseth) for bringing the project to fruition.

The essence of spirituality is loving God. The Bible, the Talmud, and the Qur'an all direct their followers not merely to believe in God, to trust God, to obey God, or to serve God . . . but to *love* God. Spirituality may be *more* than this, but it can be nothing *apart* from this.

Many people today seem to be interested in becoming "more spiritual," and there is an abundance of spiritual advisors who help people with their inner lives. Oprah Winfrey has featured a regular segment on her television program called "Caring for Your Spirit." As near as I can tell, she and others like her offer good tips for pursuing the spiritual life (for becoming "more spiritual"). Yet I want to say this: *when caring for the spirit, do not neglect the heart*. What your spirit needs most is to love. Our spirits, our innermost beings, our true selves, yearn to love the God who made them. Satisfying spirituality, I believe, is found when the spirit and the heart come together as one and our innermost being is imbued with the capacity for adoration and ardor that the heart is so adept at providing.

When people say that they want to be "more spiritual," what exactly do they mean? They probably have some idea regarding how spiritual people talk or act or think and they want to be more like that themselves—but there's more. They want to be changed *within*. They don't just want to copy the way

1

spiritual people act or talk or think; they want to *be* spiritual people them-selves, transformed from the inside out. What they want, I think, is to love God. Richard Foster says that true spirituality "comes not from gritting our teeth but from falling in love."[1] The *reason* spiritual people act and talk and think the way they do is that they love God. Becoming people who love God is the only reliable path to being more spiritual. Loving God transforms people from within and connects them to something eternal and ultimate.

People also say that they want inner peace. They feel disconnected from a world where so much seems to be superficial. The routines and rituals of daily life become ways of passing time while something deep within yearns for life to be more meaningful. There is an element of fear. The *most* mean-ingful aspects of our lives are often our relationships, and these are fragile. Friendships sour, marriages end. People move away and lose touch. And people die. Even people we care about and depend upon. They die, and someday we will die. So how can our hearts find peace? The Bible speaks of a peace that "surpasses all understanding" (Philippians 4:7) and of a joy that yields contentment in all circumstances (Philippians 4:12-13). Such joy and peace are the result of loving God, a consequence of being in a relationship with a God whom we have come to know as a real being who inspires our devotion and affection.

For Christians, such devotion is often directed to Jesus Christ, through whom God is made known.[2] Christians may describe themselves as people who "follow Jesus" or who "believe in Jesus"; such expressions, however, can be euphemisms for what they really mean but avoid saying because the lan-guage is so intimate. Christians are people who *love* Jesus. Indeed, the Bible practically *defines* Christians as people "who have an undying love for our Lord Jesus Christ" (Ephesians 6:24).

The Christian faith is not just a religion (a system of rituals and beliefs), but a *relationship*—a relationship of love with Jesus Christ who is risen from the dead. When this basic point is missed, the Christian religion becomes hol-low and staid. Jesus warned against a day when the love of many would grow cold (Matthew 24:12) and, in a memorable passage from the book of Revelation, he told a church, "I know your works, your toil and your patient endurance . . . but I have this against you, that you have abandoned the love you had at first" (Revelation 2:2, 4). When Christianity is not, first and fore-most, a relationship of love, it becomes a matter of works and toil and patient endurance—all worthwhile, perhaps, but a far cry from the spiritual experi-ence of joy and peace that it is supposed to be.

But how do we do it? Love God? Love Jesus? How do we even know whether we are doing it or not? Can we direct the ways of our heart? Can we *learn* to love? There are many good books by Christians that deal with faith as a relationship with Jesus, books written from many different perspectives (liberal/conservative, Protestant/Catholic, and so on). Billy Graham talks about *accepting* Jesus, Marcus Borg about *meeting* him (again, for the first time). I am more concerned with *loving* him. How do we do that?

People who love God claim that they are in a spiritual relationship with the Lord and Creator of the universe. People who love Jesus say that they are in a spiritual relationship with the Son of God who lived, died, and rose from the dead. Such claims may strike many people as odd or even as fanatical, and sometimes the people who make such claims are not ideal role models, not the sort of people we would want to be. Still, there is something undeniably appealing about it—the notion of being in a *relationship* with God or Jesus. We should at least note what the Bible says about those who love Jesus and the God whom Jesus makes known: they are loved *back* (John 14:21; 16:27); indeed, they inevitably come to discover that God has loved them *first* (1 John 4:19).

# CHAPTER ONE

# Naïve Again

I think I should begin with what some religious traditions call "personal testimony." Much of what I have to say in this book is shaped by my own experience. Readers whose story is similar to mine may be able to relate all the more to what follows. Others may need to make adjustments, though I hope that even where the personal distance is great, there will be something to interest, amuse, and maybe even inspire any reader interested in the advertised topic.

I am a Lutheran Bible professor who has discovered the profundity and now enjoys the reality of what philosopher Paul Ricoeur terms "a second naïveté." One cannot have a second naïveté without a first—and so my story.

I was brought up mainly in Texas and was raised as good a Lutheran as one can be in that state. Having been baptized as an infant, I attended church every Sunday with my family, went through confirmation classes in early adolescence, participated actively in our youth group (the Luther League), and became committed at a young age to being a minister.

Why did I want to be a minister? Well, I believed in God and everything the church taught, but mainly I wanted to do the kinds of things that I figured ministers did: visit the sick, help the poor, comfort the afflicted, be a friend to those in need. This was the sixties, when love and peace were popular concepts, and ministers seemed like peaceful, loving people. I certainly didn't want to go into business (join the establishment) and make a living by trying to sell things to people. Plus, everyone liked the pastor. I thought it would be nice to have the sort of job that made everyone like you. Of course, there was a lot I did not know. I did not know that ministers often spend a lot of time with administration (adjudicating budgets, supervising staff, recruiting and training volunteers, planning building programs). They actually are involved in a business that is concerned with selling things (ideas, programs) to people. I also did not appreciate the extent to which ministers must sometimes do things that make them unpopular, often with the very people they care about the most.

Still, I was intrigued by theology. While yet in high school, I read books by Erich Fromm, Paul Tillich, and Dietrich Bonhoeffer. I got a paperback copy of the New Testament called *Good News for Modern Man* and tried to read that, starting with the Gospel of Matthew. I got sort of hung up on the Sermon on the Mount, especially the part where Jesus says it is sinful just to think about certain things even if you don't actually do them (Matthew 5:21-30). This did not seem fair. Feelings of sexual desire or anger are natural, I thought, and if God does not want us to have such feelings, then God should not make us the way we are. It isn't fair for God to give us such feelings and then tell us it is wrong to have them.

This was the late sixties and as the turbulence of those troubled but wonderful years swirled about me, it seemed that just about everything was related to religion. The civil rights movement was, to me, a social crusade for justice on the part of preachers (like Martin Luther King Jr. and my two pastors) and their motivated followers (like my parents). Protests of the Vietnam War—or, at least, of the inexcusable loss of life that it entailed—often originated within the church and were led by persons motivated by their Christian faith. At that time, Christians were generally associated with issues of substance that were matters of concern to all people who *cared*. When you heard on the news that some prominent Christian leader had said something, you didn't have to cringe and wonder if he (or she, but usually he) was speculating that a cartoon character might be secretly gay. More often, it had something to do with feeding the hungry, protecting the innocent, saving the environment, or simply promoting the values of faith, hope, and love. It didn't seem, to me at least, that Christianity was *part* of the establishment.

Christians were people who *cared*. The antithesis to Christianity seemed to be apathy. The church was one of the only places where one could engage in genuine dialogue. It was an opinionated time, but the only outlawed opinion in my church was "not caring." We had lively discussions in our Sunday school classes and Luther League meetings about drugs, racial integration, the sexual revolution, women's liberation, and so forth. No one pretended to have all the answers and no one seemed to be on a crusade to get everyone else to adopt his or her view. It was as if we were all on a quest for truth and realized that even the most outlandish viewpoint might be worthy of consideration.

Music was flowing into the church too. Guitars were not normally welcome in the sanctuary, but they were omnipresent at youth retreats and summer camp programs. We all learned the spiritual songs of Bob Dylan, Simon and Garfunkel, and Peter, Paul, and Mary, and then went on to discover a lexicon of folk rock unknown to the world at large. A Roman Catholic composer named Ray Repp wrote dozens of songs that had the same sound as material by those just-named artists, but that dealt with specific matters of the Christian faith: "I Am the Resurrection," "Allelu!," "Hear O Lord." We sang all of these songs, plus Peter Scholtes's "They'll Know We Are Christians By Our Love." Though it may seem strange today, in that time and place (with *Jesus Christ Superstar* and "Oh Happy Day" all over the radio), church was a hip place to be.

## Obsessive Joy

In retrospect, I would have to say that when I entered college in the fall of 1971, I was a very *religious* person. It never even occurred to me that first Sunday away from home not to get up and go to chapel. That was what Christians did, and being "a Christian" was as much a part of my identity as being "male" or "American" or "heterosexual." I was not just a Christian: I was a devout one. Even if I did have some arguments with the Sermon on the Mount, I was still a member of the club and, in that sense, very religious.

Then I met Jesus. If you are fifty or older, you may recall that he was getting around. If you are younger, perhaps you have nevertheless read about an odd phenomenon called "the Jesus movement." Millions of young people all over America (and beyond) were suddenly claiming to have had some sort of personal encounter with the principal object of the Christian faith. "It's not just a religion," they announced on bumper stickers and on metal buttons that they pinned to their clothing (a fad at the time). "It's a *relationship* with Jesus!" What exactly did that mean? Everyone who was part of "the movement" seemed to know, but those who were not part of the movement were left out. "No one can explain it," the insiders would say. "You just have to *experience* it."

I describe this experience as "meeting Jesus" in order to use the vernacular of the movement and of the time. What I should say is that I came to *love* Jesus in a new and unexpected way. I do not imagine that I had not already been in a genuine relationship with Jesus Christ for those years of my life prior to this new experience. I did not discover faith in the fall of 1971: I discovered piety. Still, *that* was something new, and my faith suddenly became more vital, dynamic, relevant, and thrilling. It was as though I had known only prose and discovered poetry, or had only read lyrics and now heard them sung. I felt like Dorothy opening the door of her black-and-white home upon a realm of color, or like that lucky actor in *The Purple Rose of Cairo* who discovers he can step down from the movie screen and live in three dimensions. I'm speaking not of conversion but of maturation, and this was my spiritual puberty. I discovered the difference between religion and relationship, and it *is* hard to explain. It is something like the difference between observation and astonishment, between being convinced and being amazed. It is the difference between believing something and loving someone. Indeed, the spiritual experience of being in a relationship with Jesus Christ does not feel quite like anything else, but it feels *something* like a romance, which may account for the sensuality of the metaphors that are often used to describe it. So, when I say that I met Jesus, I mean that I fell in love with him. I fell into a relationship of love with Jesus Christ, who is risen from the dead.

> When I say that I met Jesus, I mean that I fell in love with him.

The Jesus movement went on for several years, though the media (and the general public) tired of the novelty after a few months. In ecclesiastical terms, it was a "revival," a seemingly spontaneous phenomenon in which a large segment of an entire generation embraced—but also transformed—inherited patterns of religious and spiritual devotion. On the one hand, the troubled youth of the sixties seemed to be discovering en masse that certain aspects of Christianity could bring order and meaning to their chaotic and often desperate lives. On the other hand, these hippies and hippie wannabes were not about to settle for "religion as usual," and they infused the traditional faith with heavy doses of sixties idealism, anti-institutionalism, and radical individualism. They also brought guitars into sanctuaries and initiated what would become a much-maligned new genre of music: Christian rock.

The significance of the Jesus movement has, in my mind, been under-estimated historically, sociologically, and theologically. Only recently have church historians (much less their secular counterparts) begun to realize that the conversion of millions of America's teenagers to a conservative, evangelical expression of Christianity may have had ramifications beyond the novelty of ocean baptisms, religious bumper stickers, and that ubiquitous one-way hand sign. I'm not so foolish as to think I can explain alternative routes that history might have taken, but it seems likely that if there had not been a Jesus movement, many things would be different today. The more noticeable ramifications in mainline churches may be liturgical: repetitive praise choruses on the one hand and a rediscovery of dormant biblical practices on the other. The youth who were caught up in the Jesus movement were into all kinds of things—*orans* prayer (with hands uplifted), anointing with oil, laying on of hands, passing of the peace, foot washing—a decade before liturgical reform movements officially reintroduced such seemingly exotic (but actually ancient) practices to average churchgoers. But there's more to it than that: the burgeoning of organizations like Moral Majority and Promise Keepers, the election of Jimmy Carter, the murder of John Lennon, the rise of U2, the decline of Bob Dylan . . . How one sociological phenomenon can account for so many different cultural realities is a story that needs to be told. But, for now, rather than analyze or describe or evaluate the movement itself, let me just say that I was very much a part of it. If you look hard enough, you can find my picture in that cover story *Life* magazine did on the Jesus movement in the summer of 1972.

They called us "Jesus freaks" and we usually liked it. It was meant as an insult, but we called ourselves that too. The term had double meaning. At that time, the word *freak* was often used to refer to a person's primary passion: a football freak was someone who *really* loved football, and a music freak was someone who was *really* into music. This use of the term actually seems to have derived from the drug culture, where terms like "acid freak" or "pot freak" were used to specify a hippie's drug of choice. In any case, young Christians called themselves "Jesus freaks" in the early seventies to identify themselves proudly as persons who were *really* into Jesus, who loved Jesus more than anything else. Of course, those who were not a part of the revival often thought that such people were just kooks or oddballs and, for them, the term "freak" retained its traditional connotation.

Those who demeaned the Jesus freaks in the manner just mentioned were often right in their observations. For one thing, religious revivals always hold a certain attraction for people who are emotionally insecure and/or mentally unstable. Like all revivals, the Jesus movement endured its share of extremism; some of its more visible proponents behaved in outlandish ways, and a few of its subgroups morphed into curious cults that had little to do with traditional Christianity. But there is also another way in which the Jesus freaks in toto may rightly have been viewed as kooks or oddballs. Christianity has always claimed that there is an inherent foolishness to the gospel (1 Corinthians 1:18), a paradoxical element of God's revelation that runs counter to the conventional wisdom of humanity. "My thoughts are not your thoughts," God said, already in the Old Testament, "nor are your ways my ways" (Isaiah 55:8). And Jesus just made it worse: "Those who want to save their life will lose it" (Mark 8:34); "Whoever wants to be first must be last of all and servant of all" (Mark 9:35); "Love your enemies and pray for those who persecute you" (Matthew 5:44). On the surface, such declarations do not appear to be the pronouncements of a rational man. So, if the prophets and Jesus were viewed as kooks and oddballs, perhaps it is only appropriate that their followers be viewed that way as well. The apostle Paul used to delight in calling himself "a fool for Christ," which may be just a first-century way of saying "Jesus freak" (1 Corinthians 4:10).

What did it mean to be a Jesus freak? I read the Bible daily, often for hours at a time, not because I thought I should but because it brought me such pleasure. I gathered with friends almost every night and we sang songs and prayed. We spoke in tongues and felt the Spirit move us. Jesus was my best friend. He was with me all the time, everywhere I went, and I was constantly aware of his presence. The experience was one of obsessive joy.

Joy, but also obsession. Having raised children, I have since become acquainted with what can be described as adolescent (or preadolescent) fixations. Transformers, dinosaurs, Nintendo, Beanie Babies, and the like have sometimes appeared to carry powers of attraction beyond their intrinsic or logical appeal. I recall a preadolescent girl (not my own) who went through a temporary obsession (circa 1997) with the pop band Hanson. If one were to tell her, "We're going to the zoo on Monday," or "The cat is going to have kittens," she would look at you with glazed-over eyes as if to ask, "What does that have to do with Hanson?" And, "If it doesn't have anything to do with Hanson, why are you wasting my time telling me this?" That's sort of how I was with Jesus. There wasn't room or time or energy in my life for anything that was not directly and obviously related to him. I did not want to waste any of my brain cells thinking about anything but Jesus.

Back then I thanked Jesus for every good thing that happened to me. There were no coincidences. When I found a good parking space, I knew Jesus had arranged it—just for me. Logically—much less, theologically—such thinking makes no sense. Not too long ago, I heard a comic on cable television talking about athletes who like to "thank Jesus" after they win the big game. Just once, he said, wouldn't you like to see the camera go into the locker room of the *losing* team and hear somebody say, "We would have had 'em if not for Jesus! Did you see how he was helping them out there!" But during my days of obsessive joy I never thought about things like that. I never thought about *blaming* Jesus when things didn't go right.

# Out of the Closet

Pastors and others who are theologically educated know how hopelessly naïve religious obsessions can be. They are to true faith what romantic infatuation is to true love: a beginning phase, perhaps, but in need of mature development. Well, I *did* get the development. I majored in theology at Texas Lutheran College. I went on to seminary. I served as pastor at a couple of churches and then I went on to doctoral studies and earned a Ph.D. I wrote books, I attended conferences, and (I think) became someone who appears to be somewhat sophisticated in matters of theological thought. As I went through this process of development, I realized that my adolescent infatuation with Jesus was something that I was supposed to outgrow. But do you know what? It never went away. It just got shoved underneath, buried under everything else. I became a closet Jesus freak, in that I knew how to act like someone who was theologically sophisticated, but in reality I still *loved* Jesus in what seemed to be a most unsophisticated way.

So now I'm out of the closet. I got tired of pretending. I don't just believe in Jesus: I *love* Jesus, and I guess I sometimes exhibit that love in ways that test the conventions of polite society. A few years back, at one of the academic conferences that are the stuff of my professional life, a group of professors were discussing some esoteric topic on which I had once delivered a paper. Somebody made a reference to my work in support of their argument. "Powell?" an opponent responded. "Powell is just an educated Jesus freak!" The comment got a good laugh and when it got back to me, I took no offense. I just thought, well, I guess I am out of the closet after all. None of these professors knew anything about my life story or the testimony I've just related.

Still, they *saw* what I could not hide. And due to the memorable character of that one academician's outburst, I've been joshingly referred to as "the educated Jesus freak" in some circles ever since. I like it.

Now I must quickly add that *loving Jesus* is a broad concept. People express their love for Jesus in different ways, with varying degrees of emotion, commitment, disclosure, and zeal. I do not really think that I love Jesus more than my professional colleagues do. What comes to the fore, rather, is a certain brand of piety that differentiates me (and Christians like me) from persons who seem to relate to Jesus in other ways. I am comfortable with my own piety, but I do not tout it as superior to anyone else's. I don't imagine (at least not anymore) that my personal expression of faith is more genuine than that experienced by other Christians.

I embrace what Paul Ricoeur calls "the second naïveté." For me, this describes what can happen when a person *chooses* to be naïve, with full knowledge of more sophisticated, nonnaïve options. I do not regard this as stubbornness or anti-intellectualism, but as humble acknowledgment that the heart sometimes knows truth that the head does not fully comprehend. Still, to speak of a *second* naïveté does imply growth. One does not (or should not) simply revert to an earlier phase of life, rejecting everything learned in the interim. Thus, I shall devote the rest of this book to describing ways in which my understanding of what is popularly called *spirituality* has developed over the years.

The chart on page 12 previews some of the growth stages that I have observed in my own spiritual journey. We have begun to look at one of these already—the realization that spirituality means not just believing in God but *loving* God, and that such love cannot be adequately expressed with the prosaic language of theology and doctrine. It requires also the poetic voice of piety, which gives expression to the heart. These points will be discussed more  fully in the next chapter, and then we will move on to other realizations, other discoveries, other moments of growth and maturity. Your journey may be different from mine. You may be way ahead of me at some points, or you might have found that the process of discovery worked differently for you. The point of going public with my own testimony is not to provide anyone with a role model for spiritual maturity. It is just one story among many, but in discovering how we are alike and how we are different, you might just stumble upon some reference points for making sense of your own life with God. Let's hope so. In fact, let's do more than hope. Let's pray:

*Oh God, you have made us for yourself.*
*We seek you, to know you and to love you.*
*Guide us through the meager words of this little book.*
*Alert us to what is right, shield us from what is wrong.*
*Be our Guide. Be our Vision. Be our Journey. Be our Goal.*
*You are the destination and you are the way,*
*For all true wisdom comes from you and in you we find our home.*

|  | First Naïveté | Second Naïveté | read about this in ... |
|---|---|---|---|
| Spiritual love is expressed with | the certainty of prose | the beauty of poetry | Chapter 2 |
| Spiritual understanding is grounded in ... | an internal witness | an external reality | Chapter 3 |
| Spiritual relationships are experienced as ... | intensely personal | profoundly corporate | Chapters 4–5 |
| Spiritual life is marked by ... | compulsive happiness | confident sadness | Chapter 6 |
| Spiritual hope is sustained through ... | intellectual speculation | intuitive expectation | Chapters 7–9 |
| Spiritual growth is dependent upon ... | human commitment | divine grace | Chapters 10–12 |
| Spiritual truth is presented as ... | clear and consistent | ambiguous and contradictory | Chapter 13 |
| Spiritual devotion is a matter of ... | heartfelt sincerity | faithful duty | Chapters 14–17 |
| Spiritual joy is found in ... | worldly detachment | worldly involvement | Chapters 18–19 |

# CHAPTER TWO

# The Poetry of Faith

What does the Bible say about loving Jesus? Well, it's *for* it, not *against* it—that should come as no surprise. But there's more to the matter than that.

Ephesians 6:24 refers to Christians as people "who have an undying love for our Lord Jesus Christ." First Peter 1:8 addresses believers with the assurance that "although you have not seen [Jesus], you love him." Several passages of Scripture refer to the Christian church as the "bride" of Christ (Mark 2:19; Ephesians 5:31-33; Revelation 21:2, 9; 22:17), likening the relationship between believers and Jesus to that of a couple at their wedding or, indeed, on their honeymoon.

Negatively, a *failure* to love Jesus or God is regarded not simply as a regrettable lack of reverence but as a fundamental problem that threatens to undermine everything else. We could illustrate this with numerous examples. Here's one: it is widely known that the Bible says, "the love of money is the root of all evil" (1 Timothy 6:10 RSV), but *why* is that so? Is it because people who love money tend to be dishonest or to compromise their principles in order to become wealthy? That might sometimes be true, but it doesn't seem to be the main point. Jesus claims that loving *money* gets in the way of loving *God*. "Where your treasure is, there your heart will be also," he says (Matthew 6:21).

The problem is not *having* money but *loving* it, and the reason this is a problem is that one cannot simultaneously be devoted to both God and mammon (Matthew 6:24). For Jesus, the issue is not just a question of what one does with one's money or what one does to obtain it (though these are significant matters also). Jesus is concerned about a fundamental matter of the heart: the question of whom (or what) one *loves.*

This fundamental concern is consistent throughout the Gospels. Jesus castigates the religious leaders of his day for attending to minor matters while neglecting what is most important: loving God (and honoring justice; Luke 11:42). He confronts people who are trying to kill him with a charge that he regards as more serious than their murderous intent: "You do not have the love of God in you" (John 5:42). He tells complacent believers, "If God were your Father, you would love me" (John 8:42). He draws an unfavorable comparison between a respectable cleric and a notorious sinner, insisting that someone who needs to be forgiven much and "loves much" is preferable to someone who needs to be forgiven little and "loves little" (Luke 7:44-47).

Positively, loving God or loving Jesus is presented as a fount of other virtues (including "honoring justice"; Luke 11:42). The first and greatest commandment, Jesus says, is to "love the Lord your God with all your heart and with all your soul and with all your mind." This one leads naturally to a second ("love your neighbor as yourself"). Everything else in the law and the prophets depends on these two commands (Matthew 22:37-40). This is no doubt the thinking behind St. Augustine's famous comment that the Christian life can be summarized in one phrase: "love (God) and do what you will" (*Homily on Johannine Epistles* vii, 8). If one truly loves God, then one will also love others (see 1 John 4:20), and all the desirable aspects of Christian morality and character will come naturally as expressions of a transformed heart. If you *truly* love God, you may simply "do what you will," for the desires of your heart will be virtuous, honorable, and pure.

> Loving Jesus is presented as a worthy goal in and of itself. It is not a means to an end: it is the end. It is the essence of spirituality, the defining characteristic of a person who is in a relationship with the God made known to us through Jesus.

What do people who love Jesus do? According to the New Testament, they live in a way characterized by "an indescribable and glorious joy" (1 Peter 1:8). They keep Christ's commandments (John 14:15, 21; 1 John 2:5; 5:3) and are attentive to his word (John 14:23, 24). They feed his sheep (John 21:15-17). They serve the saints (Hebrews 6:10) and love all of God's children (1 John 4:20—5:2). From such passages, we might conclude that people who love God or Jesus are expected to be happy, well-behaved, wonderful persons. Eventually, we'll have to look at why it doesn't always work out that way. For now, though, I want to stress that the Bible is not just interested in "loving Jesus" as a means to an end. The point is not simply that loving Jesus motivates Christians to do good deeds or helps them to develop appealing personalities. There is more to it than that. Loving Jesus is presented as a worthy goal in and of itself. It is not a means to an end: it *is* the end. It is the essence

| Loving God | Loving Jesus |
|---|---|
| "You shall love the Lord your God with all your heart and with all your soul and with all your mind. This is the greatest and first commandment."<br>Matthew 22:37-38<br>cf. Deuteronomy 6:5 | "Grace be with all who have an undying love for our Lord Jesus Christ."<br>Ephesians 6:24 |
| "Love the Lord, all you his saints."<br>Psalm 31:23 | Jesus to Peter: "Do you love me?"<br>Peter: "Yes, Lord; you know that I love you."<br>John 21:15, 16, 17 |
| "The Lord watches over all who love him."<br>Psalm 145:20 | "Although you have not seen [Jesus Christ], you love him; and even though you do not see him now, you believe in him and rejoice with an indescribable and glorious joy."<br>1 Peter 1:8 |
| "Be very careful, therefore, to love the Lord your God."<br>Joshua 23:11 | Jesus to the church in Ephesus: "I have this against you, that you have lost the love you had at first."<br>Revelation 2:4<br>cf. Jeremiah 2:2 |
| "All things work together for good for those who love God."<br>Romans 8:28 | |
| "No eye has seen, nor ear heard, nor the human heart conceived, what God has prepared for those who love him."<br>1 Corinthians 2:9 | Jesus to his disciples: "Those who love me will keep my word, and my Father will love them, and we will come to them and make our home with them."<br>John 14:23 |

of spirituality, the defining characteristic of a person who is in a relationship with the God made known to us through Jesus.

The Bible promises many benefits to those who love God. "Anyone who loves God is known by him," the Bible says (1 Corinthians 8:3). The Lord watches over those who love God (Psalm 145:20). All things work together for good for those who love God (Romans 8:28). Those who love the Lord will receive "a crown of life" (James 1:12) and be heirs of a kingdom (James 2:5). Frankly, we're not quite sure what all of this means. Indeed, we read that no human heart has yet conceived of the glories that "God has prepared for those who love him" (1 Corinthians 2:9)—which means the benefits of such devotion lie literally beyond our comprehension.

## Getting Sentimental

I sat in a church on the First Sunday in Advent and listened to a pastor pray: "As we prepare for Christmas this year, O Lord, help us to avoid the commercialism and the sentimentality that our society attaches to this season." I didn't say "Amen."

Sentimentality? The *commercialism,* I get. Shopping orgies are not, perhaps, the most appropriate rituals for celebrating the birth of one who said, "Life does not consist in the abundance of possessions" (Luke 12:15). But *sentimentality?* Since when is sentimentality a bad thing, something we must pray for God to help us avoid? Isn't Christmas a season of love—and isn't *love* by its very nature sentimental?

Well, yes and no. The first thing we need to say about love—perhaps the most important thing—is that the Bible describes love in terms of behavior, not emotion. Love is something you *do,* not just something you *feel.* We see this, for instance, in 1 Corinthians 13 (a favorite wedding text): "Love is patient; love is kind; love is not envious or boastful or arrogant or rude. It does not insist on its own way; it is not irritable or resentful" (verses 4–5). The very notion of love as a *commandment* assumes this as well. It would make little sense for Moses or Jesus or anyone else to command people to *feel* a certain way. How would we obey, even if we wanted to? Can we control our feelings? So, when the Bible says "Love your neighbor," it does not mean that we have to *like* our neighbor or enjoy our neighbor's company: it means we ought to treat our neighbor in ways that are patient and kind, not envious or boastful or arrogant or rude . . . and so on.

This is certainly true of loving God as well. We love God best through our behavior, by worshiping God and living the way God wants us to live. Still, there is more to it than that. There is also *delight*. Those who love God take delight in the Lord (Psalm 37:4); they even take delight in living the way that God wants them to live (Psalm 40:8). Emotions will wax and wane, of course, but there is absolutely nothing wrong with feeling emotional about our relationship with God—indeed, there is probably something wrong with *never* feeling that way.

A few years ago, a student in one of my seminary courses began a class project by playing a song by some contemporary Christian singer on an old and soon-to-be-outdated cassette deck. The song was one of those maudlin numbers—a love song to Jesus, in which the singer sounded like he thought Jesus was his girlfriend, his *junior high school* girlfriend, to judge by the sappy lyrics and simplistic rhyme scheme. This was being played in a room full of serious theology students, more than one of whom I could tell were trying to suppress their laughter as one trite cliché after another poured out of the creaky speaker in mawkish swells of vocal exhibitionism. I think we all assumed the student intended the piece as a bad example of liturgical excess or something like that, on which she would comment in time. But as the song ended, there were tears streaming down her face and we all realized, suddenly, that she had been deeply moved by what we had been ready to mock. Now we felt guilty—at least I did. There was nothing really wrong with the song—it was just so . . . sentimental.

> There is absolutely nothing wrong with feeling emotional about our relationship with God—indeed, there is probably something wrong with never feeling that way.

There's no accounting for taste, of course, but this student was an intelligent and sophisticated person. She was pursuing a master's degree in religion, and yet she could be reduced to tears by the emotionalism of a simple "love song to Jesus." Personally, I do not think that makes her any less sophisticated: I think it makes her well rounded. We are to love God with our heart and mind. We demonstrate that love through actions, with behavior and commitment that remain consistent even when our feelings fluctuate (as they always do). But we are whole persons: love is also something that we feel, at least sometimes, and I cannot help but think that God is pleased with the vulnerability that allows such feelings to be expressed.

I know the power of a sentimental song. I used to choke up when Bobby Goldsboro sang "Honey." Of course, that was 1968 and I was only fifteen. By the time Bob Carlisle did "Butterfly Kisses" (1997), I had grown (somewhat) impervious to such tugs at the heartstrings. But is that something to be proud of? It's nice, I suppose, to feel that one is not easily taken in, not subject to having one's emotions manipulated in obvious and predictable ways. But are we better people, do we have better lives, is our love somehow more pure, when we succeed at shielding our emotions from these influences? Not to be manipulated is one thing; not to be aroused, inspired, affected, or simply "touched"—well, that's another.

Martin Luther, at any rate, didn't worry too much about avoiding the sentimentality of the Christmas season. He wrote a hymn called "From Heaven Above To Earth I Come," which, like most of his hymns, is quite stately and very theological. At least it starts out that way. As it goes along, it gets less stately, as if there was something about that baby in a manger that just, you know, got to him. Stanza twelve has really sappy lyrics:

> O dearest Jesus, holy child,
> Prepare a bed, soft undefiled,
> A holy shrine, within my heart,
> That you and I need never part.

## A Lost Virtue

There is a religious term that describes well the holistic combination of "love as behavior" and "love as emotion," of "living as God would have us live" and "taking delight in the Lord." Unfortunately, it is a term that has fallen on hard times and does not seem to be too popular any more. The word is *piety.* Most people I know want to be "spiritual"; most do not want to be "pious." I almost never hear the latter word used positively. When a politician refers to "the pious platitudes of my opponent," I know he does not mean this as a compliment.

Why is this? The very concept of *piety* summons unfortunate images in people's minds. To some, it is almost a synonym for hypocrisy: pious people are frauds who don't practice what they preach. More often, it suggests a superficial veneer of religion that is out of touch with reality: pious people are simpletons who believe God will solve all their problems. Or, frequently, the term summons images of judgmental intolerance: pious people are annoying moralists who think they know how everyone else should live. For modern Americans, a list of people who are "pious" might include Ned Flanders from *The Simpsons* and an assortment of television evangelists.

I will not defend hypocrisy, superficiality, or intolerance, but I will defend the fundamental concept of piety. The word *piety* literally means "duty" or "faithfulness" (from Latin *pietas*), and it is typically used with reference to those who feel a duty toward God and who try to be faithful in fulfillment of that duty. Above all, pious people believe that human beings should love God, and they try their best to do that. Some pious people are judgmental, superficial, or hypocritical, though I doubt that they are this way *because* of their piety. If they weren't pious, they would be judgmental, superficial, or hypocritical people who didn't try to love God, as opposed to being judgmental, superficial, or hypocritical people who do try to love God. Being pious (or becoming pious) does not automatically remove the basic deficiencies of one's human condition, and yet people tend to notice unflattering traits in the pious precisely because they seem incongruous. Homer Simpson is at least as judgmental, superficial, and hypocritical as his neighbor Ned, but we don't notice this so much because we have no reason to expect better of him.

What I like about piety is that it effectively combines commitment and sentiment in a spiritual mélange that emphasizes the experiential dimension of faith. Despite all their fumbling, pious people (or people who want to be pious) are typically unashamed of their emotional devotion to Jesus, and yet they know better than to ground that devotion in their emotions. Their commitment to faith as something to be *experienced* prompts them to temper the emotion with an appropriate sense of obligation (duty). They do what they do (go to church, read the Bible, say their prayers) whether they feel like it or not—and yet they often *do* feel like doing such things and are not embarrassed by those feelings. There is something healthy, something appealing about this.

Still, piety is not all there is to religion or faith. The pious tend to view commitment and sentiment, emotion and behavior, as matters of the heart, as aspects of Christian *experience*. What else is there? Well, there is *theology* . . . but perhaps that doesn't interest you. Or maybe it does. Either way, this isn't primarily a theology book, but we will take just a moment to say a word about the necessary—if sometimes uneasy—relationship between piety and theology.

Throughout history, there have been struggles between Christian movements that located the authenticity of Christian faith in experience (feelings and practices) and those that emphasized doctrine, subscription to orthodox beliefs. In our modern day, the concept of *piety* is often contrasted

(• Orthodoxy vs Orthopractise)

with *theology* as "matters of the heart" versus "matters of the mind." Theology concerns itself with the doctrines and beliefs, with a correct understanding of the faith. Piety deals with feelings and attitudes and spiritual motivations. Inevitably, the two get pitted against each other in arguments over which is more important or which should receive the proper emphasis. Defenders of what is rational and true sometimes view "pietists" as anti-intellectual competitors who would demean what they hold to be important.

We are to love God with our heart *and* mind—which certainly means that "what's in the heart" is not all that counts. Loving God with our mind has myriad implications:

- We love God by learning as much as we can about Jesus, about the Bible, and about our faith, so that our devotion to God may be grounded in sound understanding.
- We love God by learning to think clearly and logically, so that we can make wise decisions not only about our religious beliefs but about our jobs, our families, and everything else.
- We love God by remaining teachable and honest, ready to evaluate our assumptions and to revise our opinions when we discover that they are wrong.
- We love God by seeking truth earnestly and without compromise, by thinking deeply about the hard questions of life and refusing to settle for easy answers.
- We love God by pursuing excellence, learning skills and acquiring knowledge that will allow us to make valuable contributions to the world in which we live.
- We love God by doing whatever we do thoughtfully and creatively, envisioning different scenarios and consequences, preparing for successes and failures, and becoming sufficiently organized to be reliable people who keep their commitments.
- We love God by remaining alert and perceptive and by keeping our goals and objectives before us, such that we might pursue a steady course even when our emotions would pull us one way or another.
- We love God by enjoying knowledge, by loving wisdom, and by fully appreciating what wonderful gifts our *minds* can be.[3]

There is enough material here for an entire book. Still, the main focus of *this* book is on the union of spirit and heart.

I do not want to exalt either theology or piety at the expense of the other. Of course, I know people who are deeply pious and yet have terrible theology. I also know people for whom the converse would be true. I think of the matter this way: *faith* is the umbrella term, and *theology* and *piety* represent two aspects of faith. I don't know which of the two is more important, and I don't really care. I don't even want to propose some bland compromise that suggests they are both "equally important." All I know is that both theology and piety are significant for faith, and that's enough for me.

Still, they are different. I like to think of theology as the *prose* of faith and piety as the *poetry*. Obviously, we need prose if we are going to communicate with each other in meaningful ways. The strength of prose is clarity: it follows rules of grammar and allows people to articulate information in a useful fashion. Poetry is less useful than prose, but it is often more beautiful. It doesn't always "make sense" in the same way that prose does, and people who don't get it (don't understand it or appreciate it) sometimes don't get it *at all*.

The same may be true of theology and piety. Good theology follows certain rules of logic and rational discourse. When a religious denomination wants to engage in ecumenical dialogues with another sect, the two groups need to compare their beliefs and confessions. They need to talk about doctrine not emotion, theology not piety. This often happens at an institutional level, and it is both important and good. Still, Christians who belong to both groups might get together and discover that they share common experiences, feelings, and spiritual motivations: "I don't even know why we're different," they might say. "We both love Jesus." Theologians can recognize that this happens and celebrate the fact without fearing that their work is jeopardized.

This is not to say that piety is all that counts. In his book *Mere Christianity,* C. S. Lewis tells of an encounter with a man who feels no need for theology. He says, "I know God because I've *felt* him." Lewis says this is a bit like a sailor saying he has no need for maps or charts because he loves the ocean and has personally experienced its power and glory. Anyone can *experience* the ocean by taking a walk on a beach, but "a map is going to be of more use than walking on the beach if you want to get to America."[4] Of course, this is correct. Still, I would pity the ship captain who possesses admirable navigational skills but feels no thrill at the smell of salt air or the sound of crashing waves.

We need theology. It is important because it is useful. Piety is less useful (less utilitarian or functional), but it is often more beautiful and, indeed, more thrilling. It ignores some of the rules theologians have to follow and so can be unpredictable and surprising.

Nevertheless, I have indicated that piety has become something of a lost virtue within our culture, an unappreciated value that is sought only by a few. So let us be honest about the journey we are on. Becoming pious will not help us to win friends or influence people. Loving God will not make us more popular or bring us worldly success. But it will make us "more spiritual": it will take us to the very heart of what spirituality is really all about.

> I like to think of theology as the *prose* of faith and piety as the *poetry.*

Piety is the poetry of our faith and the cornerstone of our spirituality. What will happen if you become a person who loves Jesus in this complicated world? Simply put, you will be *closer to God.* You will experience what it means to be in a spiritual relationship with the Lord and Creator of the universe, in fellowship with the One who lived and died and then rose from the dead.

# CHAPTER THREE

# Sense-able Spirituality

There is a sense in which I don't like the word *spirituality* very much. It seems to describe something unreal. In a popular sense, "spirit" is often contrasted with "matter" or "flesh" or, simply, with what is accessible to the senses. "Spiritual things," almost by definition, are those things that we cannot see or hear or smell or taste or touch. Accordingly, what counts as "spiritual" is often pretty vague. Eugene Peterson has described such spiritual fuzziness by indicating that our current understanding of spirituality is "transcendence vaguely intermingled with intimacy." He then defines those two terms:

*Transcendence*: a sense that there is more, a sense that life extends far beyond me, beyond what I get paid, beyond what my spouse and children think of me, beyond my cholesterol count.

*Intimacy*: a sense that deep within me there is a core being inaccessible to the probes of psychologists or the examinations of physicians, the questions of the pollsters, the strategies of the advertisers.[5]

Yes, we all long for such transcendence and intimacy but, as these very terms suggest, spirituality must then be conceived as something other than life that is accessible to our senses. A lot of people seem to like this necessary ambiguity because they can then define "what is spiritual" in terms that suit their purposes or meet their needs. But self-defined spirituality runs the risk of being the product of psychological self-projection (wishful thinking) rather than engagement with anything that is *real*.

Voltaire is reputed to have said, "If God has created us in His image, we have more than returned the compliment." There seems to be a universal human tendency for people to fashion God to their own design and so to believe in a God that they find fashionable. This tendency is the first and perhaps the greatest problem to be overcome if we want to grow spiritually. Those of us who do not overcome it, or who do not even try, may end up with a form of spirituality that seems satisfying, but it will also be one that is not challenging. And nonchallenging spirituality is only satisfying in the short term. A fashionable God will always let us down, eventually.

For many people, having a spiritual relationship with God depends largely on believing in a God who thinks and acts the way that they want God to think and act. Some people want to believe in a compassionate caregiver; others want to believe in a powerful disciplinarian. Some want a God who is helpful and who often intervenes in human affairs; others prefer a distant and unobtrusive deity who lets people figure things out for themselves. The problem with all of these conceptions is that they represent different answers to the question, "What do I want God to be like?" as opposed to "What is God really like?"

One would think that theologians would be adept at answering the latter question, and I suppose they are, but there are just too many of them. Whatever you want to believe about God, you will be able to find some theologian who will tell you that you are right (while many more tell you that you are wrong). Of course, we also have the Bible and we would be lost without it, but, again, there are lots of different perspectives expressed in the Bible and it is difficult to sort them all out. History and experience reveal that it is possible for human beings to pick certain parts of the Bible that they find to their liking and ignore the rest. And it is possible for them to do this without even realizing that they are doing it.

A primary characteristic of what I call the "first naïveté" (almost the *defining* characteristic) is believing that the world really is the way that we want it to be. Most people probably start out believing this, and if spirituality is important to them they may also begin their life of faith with an idealistic image of God appropriate to their view of the world. But then things happen and reality comes crashing in upon them. Maybe there is some major crisis, or maybe it's just the slow grind of daily observation. In any case, they eventually figure out that the world is *not* the way they want it to be, and this discovery has spiritual implications for what they believe (or at least for how they feel) about God.

Some people lose their faith. They don't necessarily become atheists, but they lose interest in having a relationship with a God who does not appear to think or act the way they want. Their spiritual development is derailed and years later they might smile in bemusement at naïve people who talk about knowing God or having a relationship with Jesus. They've been there, done that, and found that it doesn't work. But, in fact, all they really discovered is that it does not work to have a relationship with an image of God that is the product of one's own wishful thinking. "You say you lost your faith," Bob Dylan sang while I was in high school, "but you had no faith to lose."

Other people just continue on in denial, their spiritual lives unaffected by maturity in other areas. Even after they realize that the world is not as they thought or hoped, they continue to believe that God really is what they always thought God should be. Such spirituality seems divorced from reality or, at least, resistant to growth. Down the road, such people often describe their spiritual lives as stagnant: nothing moves them or inspires them quite as much as before and they look back wistfully on a time when they felt closer to God than they do now.

It's not supposed to be like that—and it doesn't have to be. The clear expectation of Scripture is that believers will *grow* spiritually and discover their relationship with God becoming more intimate and satisfying as the years go by. Paul describes the Christian life optimistically as being transformed from one degree of glory to another (2 Corinthians 3:18). How can that be? The key, I think, lies in resisting the all-too-human tendency of defining God in our own image. For me, this has been a matter of grounding spirituality in a reality external to myself.

> The clear expectation of Scripture is that believers will *grow* spiritually and discover their relationship with God becoming more intimate and satisfying as the years go by.

# The Accessible God

The focus of New Testament spirituality is the person of Jesus. That may seem obvious, but, actually, the fact is often missed. Many Christians take the focus of spirituality to be the Holy Spirit. If you check bookstores or libraries, you will find that much of what is written about spirituality within a Christian context discusses ways that the Holy Spirit is to be experienced in our lives. One can speak about the matter responsibly in that way, but I don't think that this is what any of the biblical writers would have done. The biblical authors, especially Paul, focus primarily on the continuing relationship of believers with Jesus Christ, who is risen from the dead.

To check this, you can get a good concordance and look at how many times the letters of Paul use expressions like "in Christ" or "of Christ" to describe the spiritual lives of Christians. Here is a small sampling:

- "Greet Andronicus and Junia, my relatives, who were . . . in Christ before I was" (Romans 16:7).
- "As all die in Adam, so all will be made alive in Christ" (1 Corinthians 15:22).
- "It is God who establishes us with you in Christ" (2 Corinthians 1:21).
- "We are not peddlers of God's word like so many; but in Christ we speak as persons of sincerity" (2 Corinthians 2:17).
- "If anyone is in Christ, there is a new creation: everything old has passed away; see, everything has become new" (2 Corinthians 5:17).
- "God . . . has blessed us in Christ with every spiritual blessing" (Ephesians 1:3).
- "In Christ we have also obtained an inheritance" (Ephesians 1:11).

Theologians argue about everything, so we should not be surprised to learn that they argue about the precise meaning of these words: what exactly does it mean to be *in Christ*? But I think everyone would agree on this much: the expression refers to some sort of relationship that believers are expected to have with Jesus Christ. In every verse above, we could substitute the words "in a relationship with Jesus Christ" for the shorthand expression "in Christ" without really altering the meaning.

The Bible says that God sends Jesus into the world (John 3:16) and draws people to Jesus (John 6:44). The Holy Spirit facilitates this relationship with

Jesus (John 16:14) and is sometimes even called "the Spirit of Jesus" (Acts 16:7; compare Galatians 4:6). We believe in God the Father and in God the Holy Spirit, but our spiritual lives are best understood as a relationship with Jesus that the Father establishes and the Spirit sustains.

I realize that this might seem like a pedantic point that would only be of interest to theologians, but the practical value will become evident shortly. For Christians, "being spiritual" means being in a relationship with *Jesus*— not just being in a relationship with God or with the Holy Spirit. This Jesus is a figure of historical record. Christians claim to be in a current relationship with a person who once walked this earth, died, and then rose from the dead. That is what Christians really mean when they talk about being "spiritual." They mean (whether they always realize it or not) that they are in a living relationship with a person who has been raised from the dead.

So why is this important? When we understand our spirituality as a relationship with Jesus, our spiritual lives are *grounded in a reality external to ourselves*—something that we are not able to manipulate or fashion to our own design (at least, not easily). This gives an integrity to our spirituality that basically keeps us honest. If you don't get this just yet, at least read on to the end of this short chapter. It

> To know God through Jesus is to be in a relationship with someone who has been seen, heard, and touched.

took me several years to realize why this is important and, though you may be quicker on the uptake than I was, this could still be a point that requires a few moments of pondering.

The Bible describes God as mysterious and invisible, as a reality that is not accessible to our five senses. "No one has ever seen God," the Bible says (John 1:18; 1 John 4:12). Likewise, the Bible insists that the Holy Spirit is like the wind that "blows where it chooses, and . . . you do not know where it comes from or where it goes" (John 3:8). But what the Bible says about Jesus is very different: "what we have heard, what we have seen with our eyes, what we have looked at and touched with our hands . . . we declare to you" (1 John 1:1-3). The Jesus of the Bible is God made accessible. To know God through Jesus is to be in a relationship with someone who has been seen, heard, and touched.

Our living Lord Jesus Christ now has a spiritual body. We do not see him or hear him or experience him directly through our physical senses. Still, to use Marcus Borg's terms, this *post-Easter Jesus* is still the same person as the *pre-Easter Jesus*, and this means that we can know a great deal about him.[6]

When I read in the Bible about the Jesus who worked in Galilee, I learn about the Jesus to whom I pray. I learn how he thinks, what he values, what pleases him, what makes him angry, and what makes him sad. I discover his *person-ality*. And I am able to carry all of this over into my relationship with the risen Lord whom I love, worship, and seek to serve.

# A Force with Flesh

Whatever else my relationship with Jesus Christ may be, it is not just some ambiguous, New Age thing, where I try to get in touch with a self-defined spirit of the universe. There is quite a gulf between biblical Christian spirituality and *Star Wars* spirituality ("Use the force, Luke"). *Star Wars* is great entertainment and even all the stuff about "the force" is kind of inspiring, but what about life in the real world? Christians believe that "the force" became flesh and lived among us (compare John 1:14). We believe that "the force" is a person who has a name and a personality, a person who left a historical record regarding what he said and did in this world.

When I go to the regular, general-market bookstores and look at the shelves marked "spirituality," I see many books that offer somewhat more sophisticated versions of the *Star Wars* divorced-from-reality theme. The common goals of many contemporary works on spirituality are (1) to help readers get in touch with their own spiritual nature (their individual souls), and (2) to help readers get in touch with a transcendent spiritual quality that unites all things (a life force that binds together all humanity and probably all creation). There is nothing wrong with these goals, and I am sure that many of these books help people at various stages of spiritual development. At the very least, one hopes, they bring their readers to the realization that "one's life does not consist in the abundance of possessions" (Luke 12:15).

What these books do *not* do is help readers to ground their understanding of spirituality in anything external to themselves. They depend on vagueness to allow readers to fill in the blanks with whatever they choose. Readers are allowed (indeed encouraged) to adapt the spiritual teaching to fit their own understanding of the life force, whatever that may be. Such generic spirituality does not challenge the readers' personal notions about God or souls or life forces; it does not even attempt to address the basic question of whether the readers' notions are actually correct or simply the product of wishful thinking.

And here is another concern: Is it really possible to have a relationship with something so vague and undefined as a "world soul" or a "ground of all being" or a "transcendent consciousness"? Is it possible to love an anonymous life force that has no personal presence, no distinctive demeanor, no recognizable traits or evident qualities? (In *Star Wars,* as I recall, the "force" was something one *used,* not something one *loved*). And here is an even better question: Will this product of your imagination ever love you *back*? Or even love you *first*?

As I've moved through stages of my own spiritual development, I've had to think about my relationship with Jesus in this light. A psychologist once told me that teenagers relate to Jesus in the same way that small children sometimes have an "imaginary playmate," a person they invent and talk to—and experience as quite real. Maybe my relationship with Jesus was a bit like that once, but not any longer. The Jesus I love is not just the product of my imagination. He is a figure of historical record. He lived on this earth and people wrote down things that he said and did.

That historical record puts limits on my powers of fabrication. The fact is, Jesus said things that I wish he had not said, and he did things that I wish he had not done. But I can't change that. I have to learn to love Jesus in a way that deals with all those things about him that I might not like—including the fact that he might want me to do things that I do not want to do or to be things that I do not want to be. Throughout history, Christians who have been regarded as exemplars of spirituality have testified to having relationships with Jesus that are a bit feisty at times. They have been angry and disappointed with him and they have felt his anger and disappointment with them. I'm a long way from being included in the company of these saints, but I do see that the struggles they describe are intrinsic to a spiritual relationship that will be challenging (and therefore most satisfying in a long-term sense).

I don't want to disparage any path to spiritual enlightenment or any prescription that helps people at various stages of their faith journeys. I do want to emphasize a potential strength of *Christian* spirituality that is often lacking elsewhere. The Christian claim is that a God who really does exist became accessible to us in the person of Jesus Christ. On the plane of human history (on our "turf," so to speak), God became accessible to human senses. In the person of Jesus Christ, God was seen, heard, touched, and (I presume) tasted and smelled. A spirituality that accepts this proposition is preeminently sense-able, and this peculiarly sense-able spirituality is grounded in

29

something external to ourselves, something that we cannot ultimately control or fashion to our own design.

Through Jesus Christ, God has become real and knowable in ways that we never would have expected or imagined. In fact, God becomes so real to us through Jesus that we often discover significant differences between "what God really is like" and "what we would want God to be like." The God made known to us in Jesus is not the God that we or anyone else would invent. For that reason, biblical Christian spirituality is never going to be as immediately attractive or appealing as homemade varieties that don't have to concern themselves with such pesky questions as "is this really true or is it just what I would *like* to be true?"

> The Jesus I love is not just the product of my imagination. He lived on this earth and people wrote down things that he said and did.

If Jesus really is risen, raised from the dead and living now with a spiritual body, then we can indeed have a relationship with a Jesus who is real, not just imaginary. We can come to know this Jesus and be challenged by him. We can grow to love this Jesus in ways that are both intimate and mature. And we can experience what it means to be in a reciprocal relationship with a spiritual being who loves us back—indeed, who loved us first (1 John 4:9).

# CHAPTER FOUR

# The American Way

The Gospel of Matthew concludes with the promise of the risen Lord, "Remember, I am with you always, to the end of the age" (Matthew 28:20). This may be my personal favorite verse in all of Scripture. When I was a college student, I saw it every morning chiseled into the stone walls of what the school appropriately called The Chapel of the Abiding Presence. Following the King James Version, they had it as "Lo, I am with you alway." I used to wonder why it said *alway* instead of *always* and suspected the stone-cutter of making an error. But I did stop each day and read that verse on my way to class, and it gave me inspiration to carry on. Much later, I wrote a devotional about it called "The Only Verse We Really Need." Take everything else, leave me this one passage, and I'll get by.

As near as I can tell, the age has not ended and, if this verse of Scripture be true, then Jesus must still be around, present with us somehow even today. But where? Since we don't *see* him or *hear* him—how do we actually realize his presence in ways that go beyond what might just be symbolic or imaginary?

# In the Midst

The Gospel of Matthew, in which this promise is found, also contains a few other passages that speak of the continuing presence of Jesus (see the chart on page 33). Much can be said about each of these *promises of presence*—and much has been! I only want to make two observations at this time. First, Jesus seems to connect his continuing presence in this world to fellowship with other people and to service performed on their behalf. He does not, for instance, promise to be present in nature or in the arts or in any other abstractions that do not invoke the realities of flesh and blood. Every now and then, I hear someone say, "I experience the presence of Christ whenever I see the beauty of a sunset or hear the strains of a Mozart concerto." I think I know what they mean, and I think I experience that sometimes, too (substitute Jimi Hendrix or Neil Young for Mozart), but in the Bible, Jesus says that he will be present *with* people *through* people. We encounter him when we minister to missionaries (Matthew 10:40), children (Matthew 18:5), or needy siblings (Matthew 25:40), or when we join with each other in prayer (Matthew 18:20) and share together the meal called Holy Communion (Matthew 26:26).

Second, the tenor of these references is decidedly *plural*. The *you* in Matthew 28:20 is a plural *you*, a point that may not be adequately conveyed in English translations of the original Greek. The *you* with whom Jesus promises to abide until the end of the age is a community composed of his followers and of those who are made disciples by them. This community experiences Jesus as present when it welcomes children, cares for the needy, and so forth. The emphasis of these texts is not on identifying how any single Christian might experience Jesus as present in his or her individual life. The emphasis, rather, is on how the community will experience that presence in its corporate life.

With that in mind, one phrase in Matthew 18:20 becomes especially interesting. Jesus says, "Where *two or three* are gathered in my name, I am there among them" (italics mine). This passage has a history of tongue-in-cheek application in the church. Pastors and other leaders love to quote it at poorly attended church meetings to indicate a quorum: "We may not have many here tonight, but Jesus said he would be present even when no more than two or three gather in his name, so I guess we have enough." Well, yes, but the point of the reference may not be to indicate how few it takes for his presence to be felt, but how many. It takes *at least* two or three, which is to say more than one. The presence of our risen Lord Jesus Christ is not realized in

*(possible, even one fellowship, or denomination)*

any one individual but, definitively, in the fellowship or interaction that takes place between individuals. *(the body of Christ must be in 'unity' to find*

*community.*

*—JWC.*

Of course, I am not saying that individuals do not rightly sense that God or Jesus is with them when they are alone. When the author of the twenty-third psalm claims, "The Lord is my shepherd," he testifies to a deep and abiding relationship with his God, a relationship that is intensified by that personal pronoun *my*. In fact, I have always been annoyed by liturgical purists

---

### THE PRESENCE OF JESUS IN THE GOSPEL OF MATTHEW

- **"Whoever welcomes you welcomes me, and whoever welcomes me welcomes the one who sent me" (Matthew 10:40).** Here, Jesus is saying that he will manifest himself to Israel through the twelve apostles who go out to preach and to heal in his name.

- **"Whoever welcomes one such child in my name welcomes me" (Matthew 18:5).** Here, Jesus is indicating that he will be represented in his community of followers by little children, who are the greatest in the kingdom of heaven, and by others who humble themselves and become like these children.

- **"For where two or three are gathered in my name, I am there among them" (Matthew 18:20).** Here, Jesus is promising to be with people who gather in his name to pray and who agree with one another in prayer.

- **"And the king will answer them, 'Truly I tell you, just as you did it to one of the least of these who are members of my family, you did it to me'"** (Matthew 25:40). Here, Jesus is prophesying that, at the final judgment, people who cared for members of his family when they were hungry, thirsty, alienated, naked, sick, or in prison will have those deeds rewarded as though they were performed for the Son of Man himself.

- **"Jesus took a loaf of bread, and after blessing it he broke it, gave it to the disciples, and said, 'Take, eat; this is my body'" (Matthew 26:26).** Here, Jesus is saying that his followers will continue to realize his bodily presence among them when they eat a sacred meal together in anticipation of the coming kingdom.

- **"Remember, I am with you always, to the end of the age" (Matthew 28:20).** Here, Jesus is promising to be with his followers as they go out to make disciples of all nations, baptizing people in the name of the Father, Son, and Holy Spirit, and teaching them to obey everything that he commanded.

who want to purge hymnals of songs that testify to personal faith, as though the entire congregation cannot sing such numbers as collective expressions of what its members experience as individuals. Such purges were a fad in the seventies and eighties, and, in mainline churches at least, piety would be the worse for it. In the nineties, some of the deleted songs would be restored via hymnal supplements, along with treasures these Christians had seldom sung before: "Precious, Lord, Take My Hand"; "Be Thou My Vision"; "I Want To Walk as a Child of the Light."

> The presence of our risen Lord Jesus Christ is not realized in any one individual but, definitively, in the fellowship or interaction that takes place between individuals.

So also, in the Gospel of Matthew, Jesus encourages individuals to have private devotional lives: "Whenever you pray, go into your room and shut the door and pray to your Father who is in secret; and your Father who sees in secret will reward you" (Matthew 6:6). Still, the abiding presence of the risen Christ may be something different from a personal encounter in which I experience God as one who cares for me like a shepherd or who hears my private prayers. When Jesus wants to speak of that mysterious, abiding presence, he no longer says, "go into your room and shut the door"; he says, join with others in prayer and I will be there "among them" (Matthew 18:20). Again, I first learned this verse from the King James Bible where the words "among them" are translated "in the midst of them." I still like that better, and it explains for me the difference between what I can experience of Jesus Christ's presence in my personal life and in the communal life of the church. God sees and rewards what is in secret, but when I am alone, there is no *midst* for the risen Lord Jesus Christ to inhabit. That takes (at least) two or three of us together.

A similar point is made in the Old Testament where a psalmist writes, "You are holy, enthroned on the praises of Israel" (Psalm 22:3). In church circles, this verse is often paraphrased as expressing the thought that "God inhabits the praises of God's people" (since the King James Version used the word *inhabits* instead of the more powerful *enthroned on*). In any case, we should note once more the assumption of a corporate body. Individual Israelites were always encouraged to praise God, but the presence of God (the habitation or, indeed, enthronement of God) was manifested in the worship of the full community.

Our goal is not simply locating God but *loving* God. Theological questions about "where God is found" and "how God is revealed" will only interest us if they help in that quest. But already we seem to have noticed this: *love* is a relationship, and loving God means being in a relationship with the God who has loved us first. We come to know this God through Jesus Christ who makes God accessible to us, and we come to love this God by loving Jesus Christ, through whom God's love for us is made real. The first step to being closer to God, then, is being in a relationship of love with Jesus Christ, and *that* is why what the Bible says about the continuing presence of Jesus in our world is important. If indeed that presence is located in the midst of people who pray and work in his name or even among people who are regarded as the lowliest of humans in our world ("the least of these"), then it is just possible that loving Jesus might necessarily involve loving those people in whose midst he has curiously chosen to dwell. It is even possible that loving Jesus could mean becoming part of that "midst" ourselves.

## Knocking on the Door

The central theme of the Jesus movement revival of the seventies was "a personal relationship with Jesus." This seems, indeed, to have been a connecting theme for most revivals of the last few centuries, especially those on American soil. Campus Crusade for Christ, the Billy Graham Evangelistic Association, and any number of similar organizations (for which I have the utmost respect) exhort members of their audiences to consider one all-important question: Have you accepted Jesus as your personal Lord and Savior? This, we are told, is the most important decision that any human being can ever make. It is when you "find Christ." It is when you "come to know Jesus." It is when you are "born again." It is when you "get saved." All of these momentous things happen when you pray a simple prayer and invite Jesus into your life to be your personal Lord and Savior.

What I am about to say now is a fact. It doesn't prejudge what we should or shouldn't do; it is simply a fact that ought to be acknowledged: no one in the Bible ever invites Jesus into his or her life to be his or her personal Lord and Savior—nor does Jesus ever indicate that he would come into anybody's life and be his or her personal Lord and Savior even if they were to ask him. The language itself is nonscriptural. That doesn't mean it is wrong. It just means that it's not in the Bible.

I have accepted Jesus as my personal Lord and Savior—in fact, when I was younger I did it several times. I heard someone say that this was how you found Christ, and since finding Christ seemed like a good thing to do, I prayed the prayer and accepted Jesus as my personal Lord and Savior. Then I heard someone say that it was how you came to know Jesus, and since I wasn't absolutely certain that "finding Christ" and "knowing Jesus" were the same thing, I did it again. Later I also wanted to make sure that I was born again and that I had gotten saved (which *sounded* like the same thing, but I wasn't certain), so I did it a couple more times. I guess I was sort of a conversion junkie. I didn't want to miss out on anything that God might have for me, so I prayed to accept Jesus as my personal Lord and Savior over and over again. Every time that I did this, the experience was meaningful for me, and to this day praying such a prayer (even repeatedly) strikes me as a good thing to do. Nevertheless, strictly speaking, it isn't a very *biblical* thing to do. I don't think that everything we do (even with regard to spirituality) has to have some kind of precedent in the Bible, but as I grew in faith and was taught the Scriptures I discovered that the Bible said more about how to have a relationship with Jesus than I ever would have thought of on my own—and a *lot* more than I could ever experience by just praying that prayer.

Back then, the tracts and devotional guides that told me how to ask Jesus to be my personal Lord and Savior usually quoted Revelation 3:20 (RSV) as the key verse: "Behold, I stand at the door and knock. If anyone hears my voice and opens the door I will come in to him and eat with him and he with me." I was told that this meant Jesus was knocking on "the door of my heart" and if I opened that door he would come into my heart and live inside of me. The tracts often had little drawings of a Valentine heart with a tiny chair in the middle of it. The "before" picture would show the chair empty, or worse, occupied by self or maybe even the devil. The "after" picture displayed Jesus sitting in the chair, ruling from the throne of my heart as my personal Lord and Savior.

As time went by, I got to know the Bible a little better, and I figured out that the "door" on which Jesus is knocking in Revelation 3:20 is not the door of some individual person's heart: it is the door to a church. The passage comes at the end of a discourse in which Jesus has addressed the congregation at Laodicea, upbraiding them for being "lukewarm" in their faith. Now, after speaking harshly to this church, Jesus reaffirms his desire to be present when the congregation gathers for its regular fellowship meal. He urges the church to hear his words as an invitation to repentance and says that if anyone responds to this invitation (hears him knocking and opens the door), he will come into the church and be present for its fellowship meal. I think the offer *is* quite personal: regardless of how the congregation as a whole responds, if any individual member of this errant church repents, Jesus will be present *to that person* in the communal meal. Nevertheless, the presence of Jesus is not located in an individual person's heart, but in the communal gathering of a congregation.

# The Sacrament of Decision

In America, a number of denominations and church groups seem to have made a kind of sacrament out of "personal decision." In many of these churches, every individual is urged at some point in his or her spiritual development to pray "a sinner's prayer" and invite Jesus to come into his or her heart. I am not criticizing this—I am defending it, even though it is not the practice in my own tradition. Lutherans, along with Roman Catholics, Anglicans, and other groups, generally prefer a process through which individuals are baptized as infants, instructed in the faith, and then encouraged to affirm their baptism and profess their acceptance of the faith in a ritual called Confirmation. We should quickly note that infant baptism and Confirmation are also nonscriptural rites. If it is true that no one in the Bible ever asks Jesus to come into his or her heart, it is also true that no one ever baptizes a baby or gets confirmed.

I have opinions about all sorts of things, but this book is not about Christian doctrine. I don't want to try to justify some Christian practices and denigrate others. As far as spirituality is concerned, I think it is obvious that there are people in all sorts of different churches who have come to experience a satisfying and meaningful relationship with Jesus Christ through a variety of means. People have accessed divine influences on their lives through different rites and practices. Thus, I have no problem defending and even endorsing an avenue to spirituality that is not the approach favored by my own tradition. Still, I admit that I am sometimes baffled when a group that bills itself as "a Bible church" maintains that participating in a ritual never found in the Bible is the *only* way to obtain an authentic relationship with Jesus Christ. That does seem odd, and yet it's quite common. "Have you asked Jesus to come into your heart and be your personal Lord and Savior?" the well-meaning evangelist will ask. "If not, then you aren't saved, you don't really know Jesus . . ."

I am reminded of a favorite sermon illustration that was making the rounds in the early seventies. Here is the version that appeared in a book by a popular speaker of the time, Pete Gilquist.

It's late in the second year of Jesus' public ministry, and He is teaching a group of His followers on a Judean hillside. Among those in the crowd are two men who have not met before and who happen to be seated next to each other.

While the Lord is revealing the things of God to the throng, the one man nudges the other and remarks, "Isn't He wonderful?"

"He certainly is," whispers the second. "He healed me of blindness, you know."

"He did!" says the first with surprise. "He healed me of blindness, too!"

"That's amazing," the second man remarks, motioning to his new friend to pull away from the crowd a bit so their talking will not cause disturbance. "How did it happen?"

"Well, this friend of mine—who was also blind—he and I were sitting by the edge of the road just outside of Jericho. We could tell from the voices of an approaching crowd that the Lord was coming our way and would soon pass us on the road. When he was within earshot, we yelled up to Him something like, 'Oh, Lord, Son of David, give us your mercy.' Jesus called over to us and said, 'What do you want Me to do for you?' We said, 'Lord, we just want to be able to see.' And in a flash, we both had our eyesight restored."

"Wait a minute!" says the second man, with a note of contempt in his voice. "There's no way it could have happened like that."

"What are you talking about?" replies the first.

"You've got to have *mud*," says the other. "See, first you spit into your hands, then you stoop down and get some dirt, and go to a pool and wash the mud from your . . ."[7]

For those who might not recognize the scriptural allusions, Gilquist is imagining what might have happened if one of the persons healed by Jesus in Matthew 20:29-34 had met up with the person healed by Jesus in John 9:1-7. He parodies the claim of modern Christians who sometimes say, "If you did not come to see the same way that I came to see, then as far I'm concerned, *you're still blind!*"

## Jesus and Socrates

There are Christians who would just as soon dispense with the notion of having "a personal relationship with Jesus" altogether, and I would like to direct their attention to the baby in the bathwater. There is *some* scriptural warrant

38

In the first of these passages, Paul applies the metaphor "temple of God" to the church as a whole, while in the second he appears to apply it to individual Christians. The main problem that Paul is addressing in the first part of his letter is that of divisions within the church—some people seek to follow one earthly leader, while others follow another one. So, when Paul tells the Corinthians that "God's Spirit dwells in you," he means to emphasize that the entire congregation serves as the dwelling place of God. Those who act divisively are attacking God's temple because what one does to the church, one does to God's Spirit-filled dwelling place. Later, in chapter 6 of this same letter, Paul takes the point a step further with regard to personal morality (specifically, sexual morality). An abuse of one's own body also constitutes an attack on God's temple because every individual member of the church is a part of the dwelling place that God's Spirit has filled.

My experience of growing up as a Christian in this country is that I have heard a lot of emphasis placed on the second, subsidiary point and very little emphasis placed on the main point from which it was derived. I have heard many sermons about personal morality that have sought to remind me that my body is a temple of the Holy Spirit. God dwells in each and every one of us and therefore what we do to our physical bodies we do to God's temple. We should not smoke cigarettes or overeat or abuse drugs or engage in sexual immorality. My guess is that Paul would agree with these sermons, but he would preach them only as the implications of a basic and primary point. He says to the Corinthians, your *congregation* is the temple of the Holy Spirit. God dwells in the body of assembled worshipers. What you do to *that body*—the corporate body of believers—you do to God's temple (see also 2 Corinthians 6:16; Ephesians 2:21-22). But I do not believe I have ever heard a sermon that uses the "temple of God" image in this way. I've discovered that whenever a preacher says, "Your body is the temple of God," I am going to hear a sermon about taking care of my personal, physical body—not a sermon about caring for the body of the church as a whole. In my experience, at least, the minor point tends to be stressed and the major point tends to be ignored.

If we had time to explore this further we might observe a similar tendency with regard to many other passages of Scripture. Paul tells the Corinthians, "You are a letter from Christ . . . written not with ink but with the Spirit of the living God" (2 Corinthians 3:3 RSV). I have heard sermons on this passage extolling Christians to be witnesses for Jesus in word and deed: "You may be the only Bible some people ever read—your speech and behavior must bring words of Christ to them." Yes, but Paul is actually saying that

43

the congregation at Corinth—the entire church—is a letter from Christ, bearing public witness to the world through its conduct as a community. Or, again, I grew up treasuring the promise of Scripture in Philippians 1:6, which says that the God "who began a good work in you will bring it to completion at the day of Jesus Christ" (RSV). I know that God is not finished with me yet, and I trust that God will keep working on me until at last I am done. True, but the *you* in Philippians 1:6 actually refers to the *congregation* at Philippi: God began a good work in this church and will bring that good work to completion. What the Bible teaches about churches, about communities, about congregations, no doubt applies in a secondary sense to individual Christians. Still, we are prone to grasp at this secondary meaning and overlook the main point from which it is derived.

Also: 'Living Stones' (I Peter 2:4-10) Individual, yet corporate.

## The Body of Christ

The apostle Paul also likes to describe the church as "the body of Christ," and he does so extensively in Romans 12 and 1 Corinthians 12 (see also Ephesians 1:22-23). Paul uses the metaphor to emphasize the unity of the church: individual Christians are like the many parts of one body, with Christ as the head, directing them all. The image brings out the dynamic of unity-in-diversity that seems so relevant for the church today. The many parts of the body are all different from each other, yet all are necessary. "The eye cannot say to the hand, 'I have no need of you,' nor again the head to the feet, 'I have no need of you'" (1 Corinthians 12:21).

What is most significant for our immediate purpose is that this is a strong symbol of a corporate relationship. It is the church, the community of believers, that embodies the presence of Jesus Christ in this world. No individual is ever called the body of Christ. By myself, I am only one part of that body: a hand or a foot, or an eye or an ear. Sometimes, I think I might be just a toenail or an eyelash, but no matter. Paul says that "even the members of the body that seem to be weaker are indispensable" (1 Corinthians 12:22).

According to this image, *something* of Christ may be found in me, but *all* of Christ is not found in me or in any other individual. If this is true, then I must be careful about what I mean when I say that Jesus lives in my heart. That language, meaningful and appropriate at one level, also tends to locate Christ's presence in me, and so reduces Jesus to something very small. The apostle Paul speaks in very personal terms about his individual relationship with Christ in Philippians 3:8-9, but he says there that he has counted all things as rubbish in order to gain Christ and *be found in him.* It is interesting that Paul does not say, "in order that Christ might be found in me"; instead, he says, "that I may gain Christ and be found in him." As the real estate agents say, it's all about location, location, location. Christ is big; Paul is small. Christ cannot be "found in Paul" because Christ is too big to fit into Paul's tiny little heart, but Paul can be found in Christ, as one part of Christ's body.

As I have said, the language of Jesus living in our hearts can be meaningful and appropriate. Elsewhere, Paul says, "I pray . . . that Christ may dwell in your hearts through faith" (Ephesians 3:16-17). Such language conveys the intimacy of the close, and indeed personal, connection that is desirable for every member of the church to have with Jesus Christ. The heart is the seat of love, and people who love Jesus often want to say that there is a permanent place for him in their hearts (see, for example, the hymn by Martin Luther, quoted on page 18). But the image becomes a caricature if we think that Jesus is now located within any one of us in a way that allows the relationship with him to be not merely personal but private. Paul himself can sometimes say "Christ lives in me" (Galatians 2:20), but I think he would agree with what I said above: *something* of Christ may be found in him, but since he is only one part of Christ's body, *all* of Christ will not be found in him or in any other individual. The Bible speaks positively of a personal relationship with Jesus, but not of a private relationship with Jesus.

> The Bible speaks positively of a personal relationship with Jesus, but not of a private relationship with Jesus.

American piety drifts toward a caricature that I call "the image of the Microscopic Jesus." According to this model, I invite Jesus to come into my life. He accepts my invitation, and I then have a very tiny Jesus inside me (sitting on that throne in my heart)—he has, in essence, become part of my body, and I can take him with me wherever I go. The Bible, however, offers us a different image: Jesus invites me to become part of *his* life. I accept *his* invitation and he makes me part of *his* body, taking me where *he* wants me to go. The biblical image of the body of Christ critiques the model of the Microscopic Jesus and suggests a better metaphor: rather than come into your heart and become part of *your* body, Jesus wants to draw you to his heart and make you part of *his* body. Still, as I've said, the American concept of the Microscopic Jesus is popular for a reason: it appeals to many people at a certain starting

45

point in their life of faith and seems to describe what their relationship with Jesus is like at that time. For me, at least, understanding my relationship with Jesus in terms of the biblical imagery of the body of Christ took growth and the sort of maturity associated with a "second naïveté" (see page 12).

# The Bride of Christ

In the Gospels, Jesus identifies himself as "the bridegroom" (Mark 2:19) and in Ephesians, Paul interprets marital relations as "a great mystery" that can be applied to Christ and the church (Ephesians 5:31-33). Likewise, in Revelation, the church is identified as the bride of Christ (Revelation 21:9; 22:17).

This image seems to have fallen on hard times lately (perhaps in part due to gender concerns), but I think it remains profoundly meaningful. It indicates that our relationship with Jesus is definitively a relationship of love—like that which unites a couple in marriage. Christians, according to this image, are people who are loved by Jesus Christ and who love Jesus Christ in return.

As a bit of a side note, I think the image indicates that our relationship with Jesus should be marked by profound and deep emotion, an arena of human life often dismissed as "mere sentiment" by the theologically sophisticated. The general image of "husband and wife" (in Ephesians 5:31-33) suggests lifelong love and commitment, but the specific image of "bride and groom" (in Mark 2:19) implies that our relationship with Jesus should be marked by the joyful and celebratory spirit associated with newlyweds. Brides and grooms are expected to feel a lot of emotion for each other—just look at those two in the Song of Solomon! As far I'm concerned, then, we have biblical warrant for loving Jesus in ways that sophisticated persons might dismiss as sentimental or as "silly infatuation."

But, once again, this image for a relationship with Jesus is a communal, or corporate, image. Never once in the Bible is any individual Christian identified as "the bride of Christ." Of course, individual believers are encouraged to declare their personal love for Jesus (see John 21:15-17), but there is something deeper, something more, something that the Bible calls "a great mystery" (Ephesians 5:32). There is a way, somehow, for all of us to love Jesus Christ together, presenting him with our love *as a community* and receiving in turn his love for us *as a community*. That's the mystery part. That's where it gets mystical, to use a theological term, or just sort of "spooky" in the vernacular.

Again, this thinking is not altogether new. Just for fun, I'm going to misquote a Bible passage now, and I want you to see if you can figure out what is wrong with it: "Hear, O Israelites! The Lord is our God, the Lord alone, and each of you should love the Lord your God with all of his or her heart and with all of his or her soul and with all of his or her might." Sounds a bit stilted, doesn't it? But that is in fact the way most people seem to interpret the well-known text—as a commandment to individuals. *[community -]*

Here's what the passage actually says: "Hear, O Israel: The Lord is our God, the Lord alone. You shall love the Lord your God with all your heart, and with all your soul, and with all your might" (Deuteronomy 6:4). The command is given first and foremost to the *nation of Israel*, not to individual Israelites. Of course, there is what grammarians call a "distributive sense" in which the command to the group is incumbent upon all the individuals who make up that group. There is no way for the nation of Israel to love God if the individual Israelites who compose the nation do not. Still, the directive is to the nation as a whole. What Jesus calls the "first and greatest commandment" (Matthew 22:38) is not simply for individuals to love God, but for God's people to do so *as a people*. This same concept of communal devotion carries over into the New Testament as the great mystery of love between Jesus Christ and his bride, the church.

If a lot of individuals who love Jesus get together in the same place, then we have a room full of people who love Jesus. That's nice, but it isn't exactly what the Bible has in mind. The Bible indicates that these people who love Jesus may become united in their devotion in such a way that they become a single entity. And this does not mean that they are expected to agree with each other about everything. The apostle Paul knew full well that Christians would disagree with each other on all kinds of things (Romans 14:5), but he still thought that such Christians could glorify God with a single voice (Romans 15:6—literally, the text says, "glorify God with one *mind*").

We love Jesus most purely and obviously when we worship. Many Christians indicate that as they grow spiritually, corporate, or communal, worship becomes the hallmark and highlight of their spiritual lives. That isn't always true for individuals in the early stages of spiritual development—and I'll admit that it isn't consistently true for me. Many of us feel closer to God when we engage in personal devotions or private prayer than we do in a sanctuary filled with other people. There's so much going on in the latter environment—so many distractions—and, of course, not everything is geared to our tastes. We like one song, maybe, but not the next one. Parts of the liturgy are perplexing or just plain boring. I feel that way, too, and yet . . . I do know at some level that it's not about *me*. The congregation does not gather to do things that will be pleasing or interesting to me. So I sense a potential, at least, for this worship experience to take me beyond my self-interests and involve me in an experience of loving God that is not limited by those interests.

I know that when I stand among a congregation in worship that I am part of the people who love Jesus Christ. I want to be there. I want to be part of *the people who love Jesus Christ* even when (no, *especially* when) I do not feel much love for Jesus in my own heart. And, of course, this experience of being part of the church, part of *the people who love Jesus Christ,* is a reality unbound by space or time. I am not just a part of the people who love Jesus Christ when I am in a church building on a Sunday morning. I am part of that entity—part of the bride of Christ—everywhere, all the time. Spiritual growth, for me, has meant coming to a deeper appreciation of that reality.

## A Simple Question

At the seminary where I teach, I started coming out of the closet as an unabashed Jesus freak a bit more in recent years (well, after I got tenure), and I began giving new students a sheet of paper on the first day of class that read:

Do you love Jesus?

☐ Yes

☐ No

Why or why not?

_____

_____

_____

Some people may have thought it was presumptuous or rude of me to ask incoming seminarians whether or not they loved Jesus. I just thought it was the kind of question that every Christian and certainly every pastor ought to be able to answer. Many of the students told me that no one had ever asked them this before.

You'll be happy to know that everybody checked the "Yes" box, but when it came to answering the "Why?" question, student responses were all over the place—as well they should be! I wouldn't suppose that there is a *right* answer to that question, and the questionnaire was not a pop quiz to find out how many knew what the right answer might be.

Of course, these students were at a seminary, a graduate school in theology, and so quite a few of them seemed to be intent on making sure that I would find their answer to be theologically correct. I got a lot of big words. I also got biblical and philosophical responses that were somewhat generic but no doubt heartfelt:

- I love Jesus because he is the Son of God and God is love.
- I love him because he is Lord of the universe; not to love him would be to despise life itself.

In these responses, the love seems to be based on knowledge: I love Jesus because I know that certain things are true (and, by implication, I might not love him if I did not know that these things were true).

Other students tried to craft responses that referred to their own life stories:

- I love Jesus because he has always been there for me, guiding me and protecting me. He is my Lord but also my closest friend.
- I love Jesus because he gave his life for me, that I may be forgiven my sins, and he gave me the Spirit to be my strength and comfort.

In these responses, the love seems to be based on gratitude: I love Jesus because I feel grateful to him for something that he has done for me (and, by implication, I might not love him if I did not feel that gratitude).

I would have been content to leave it at that—just noting some interesting observations about different pieties. But, naturally, a student asked me how *I* would answer the question, and I think I disappointed them all. Maybe I'll disappoint you too. Here is what I said:

- I love Jesus because I am part of the church, which is his bride. The church loves and adores Jesus, and I am part of that church so I love him and adore him also.

I think everyone thought this was a cop-out. I basically dodged the question and talked about the church rather than talking about myself. But I didn't answer like this to make some theological point about what is right or proper. It's just an honest answer. Perhaps, if I were a better Christian, I'd have a better answer. I kind of wish I did. I wish I could (honestly) say that I love Jesus because of all the philosophical things I know to be true and because of all the heartfelt gratitude I feel for him every day in response to what he has done. But it just hasn't worked that way for me. As I've gone through life, I have often become *less* confident of my own knowledge and emotions, and I really don't want my love for Jesus to be based on "what I know to be true" or "how I feel about what God has done."

My faith is not always strong, my life is not always good, and I do not always think that I am blessed. I don't want to *really* love Jesus a lot some days and only a little on other days, depending on what I think or how I feel at the time. I don't know what will happen between today and tomorrow. My faith could be shaken. All the things I'm grateful for could disappear. But I do know that tomorrow morning I'm still going to be part of the church, and the church is still going to love Jesus. So I know that I will love him too.

happy. But now I am also conscious of his absence. I have come to think that maybe Christians should always be sad. If they're not sad, how can they claim to love Jesus? Don't they miss him?

Somebody once asked me, "What does it *feel like* to be a Christian?" That seemed like an odd question, but I tried to answer. I said, "It feels like being in love with someone who has gone away." They said, "That can't be very pleasant." Well, no, I don't think it's supposed to be *pleasant,* but it is pretty powerful. I am in love with my wife, and when she is gone, I think about her constantly. I perk up at any news of her and I am energized by the slightest connection (a letter, a phone call). That's what being a Christian "feels like." Of course, it is a *confident* sadness, and we'll get to more of what that means in the next few chapters, but for now let's just admit this much: we love Jesus as a bride loves her groom, but our bridegroom has been taken away from us, and that makes us sad. The love can be real and powerful and overwhelming, but the absence is real too. And, sometimes, it's just hard.

On another occasion when Jesus was gathered with his disciples in that famous "Upper Room," a woman came in and anointed him with expensive ointment. The disciples criticized her for wasting the cologne on Jesus, saying that it "could have been sold for a large sum, and the money given to the poor." Jesus responded, "You always have the poor with you, but you will not always have me" (Matthew 26:6-11). The point was not to discourage helping the poor, but to insist that showing devotion to Jesus and concern for the poor are not mutually exclusive options. "Why do you trouble the woman?" Jesus asks, rebuking the disciples for being so contrary. When someone performs a good deed, they should not be criticized for not having performed a different good deed.

But what of that line, "You will not always have me (with you)" (Matthew 26:11)? This is the same Jesus who elsewhere says, "I am with you always" (Matthew 28:20). I have seen Matthew 28:20 printed on signs and plaques and bumper stickers. It seems to be one of people's favorite Bible verses. It is one of mine. But I don't think that I have ever seen Matthew 26:11 printed on a bumper sticker. I don't believe I have ever seen anybody needlepoint this verse and hang it in his or her kitchen. But there it is in the Bible: Jesus says, "You will not always have me with you."

Technically speaking, it is a promise. Not a command or a threat—but a promise. It is a promise of absence, an assurance that we will sometimes be "on our own." One time I was in a Christian bookstore and I saw a book called *All the Promises of the Bible.* The back cover said that there were 5,000 promises in the Bible and that this book listed them all. I checked to see if Matthew 26:11 was there, and it wasn't. So I don't know how many promises there really are in the Bible, but there must be at least 5,001.

Jesus told us that we would not always have him with us, and what he said has come to pass. He told us that the days would come when he would be taken away from us, and that has happened. Mature spirituality has to incorporate this biblical concept of the absence of Jesus along with the theme of his presence. It is not a matter of picking which of the two promises we like better—that would be a no-brainer. We have to hold the two together: Matthew 28:20 and Matthew 26:11. I made two posters with these passages on them and hung them on either side of my desk:

> Mature spirituality has to incorporate this biblical concept of the absence of Jesus along with the theme of his presence.

I will be with you always. (Matt. 28:20)

You will not always have me with you. (Matt. 26:11)

( John 14 – 17 )

## Feeding Our Impatience

On one level, the "contradiction" between these opposing thoughts is easy to understand. Jesus is still with us, but he is not with us *as he once was,* and he is not with us *as he will be.* This is why the Bible often uses language of remembrance or language of anticipation when it speaks of our relationship with Jesus.

This is never more obvious than in texts associated with the eucharistic meal, the sacred ritual through which Christians of most varieties believe they achieve some sort of "communion" with Christ and with each other. Of course, churches disagree as to exactly what this means and how it is effected, but most Christians recognize that the Bible calls them to share in such a meal, and that *something* of spiritual significance transpires when they do so. But look at some of the things that are said in the biblical accounts of Jesus instituting that meal:

- "I have eagerly desired to eat this Passover with you before I suffer; for I tell you, I will not eat it (again) until it is fulfilled in the kingdom of God" (Luke 22:15-16).

- "Truly I tell you, I will never again drink of the fruit of the vine until that day when I drink it new in the kingdom of God" (Mark 14:25; compare Matthew 26:29; Luke 22:18).
- "Do this in remembrance of me" (Luke 22:19; 1 Corinthians 11:26).
- "As often as you eat this bread and drink the cup, you proclaim the Lord's death until he comes" (1 Corinthians 11:26).
- Sacrifice –

All of these sayings seem to call attention to the ways in which Jesus will *not be present* with his disciples when they gather to eat this meal. They will eat it *in remembrance* of when he ate it with them before and in anticipation of a time when he will eat it with them again. They will eat it as people proclaiming his death. Why his death, rather than his resurrection? We know that he is risen, but when we eat this meal—a meal that he once shared with us when he was here on earth and will someday share with us again in the kingdom—we *notice his absence* and are more aware of his death than we are of his resurrection. That's how it will be, the Bible says, for people proclaiming his death "until he comes." Returns.

In light of these ways in which the meal may serve as a marker of Jesus' absence, it is interesting that Christian churches have focused so heavily on the ways in which it is a marker of his presence. This is not wrong, for his presence certainly *is* experienced. The mere fact that Jesus says we "eat his body" and "drink his blood" when we celebrate this ritual meal suggests some sort of symbolic or sacramental intimacy. Personally, I am persuaded that the presence is sacramental (not just symbolic), but I do not want to argue here for the validity of my own church's confession. I only note, somewhat ironically, that the name Lutherans use for their doctrine of Holy Communion is "real presence." We say that we believe in the "real presence" of Christ in the Eucharist (that is, the Communion meal); we almost never say that we believe in the "real absence," though that would also be scriptural and correct. Different churches disagree on how and in what way Christ is present in Holy Communion, but rarely even comment on how he is absent—a point on which, potentially, they might agree.

> Different churches disagree on how and in what way Christ is present in Holy Communion, but rarely even comment on how he is absent—a point on which, potentially, they might agree.

So if by *real presence*, we mean "actually present in a way that is not just imaginary," fine. But if we mean "really present, just as he once was with his disciples," we are wrong—the Bible encourages us to remember a time when Jesus was present with his followers in a way that he is no longer present with us now, and it encourages us to remember *that* presence with a note of sadness and longing. Or, again, if by "real presence" we mean "really present with us now, just as he will be in the future kingdom of God," we are also wrong. When the sky splits open and Jesus descends in clouds of glory and takes us up into his arms and holds us to his bosom, then, I think, we will know what the *real* presence of Christ truly is, and it will be different from what we experienced by drinking the wine and eating the bread here on earth. It will not only be different: it will be better. Experiencing the presence of Christ in the sacrament is wonderful, but it's not "as good as it gets." God has something better for us, something we cannot experience yet, something for which we wait (and yearn).

Every time we take Communion, I believe, we ought to recognize three things: (1) Christ Jesus is still present with us in a way that is real and not just imaginary: we are not just pretending he is with us—he really is with us; (2) Christ Jesus is no longer present with us as he once was—we remember when he was here on earth with us, and we miss the intimacy of that presence; (3) Christ Jesus is not now with us in the way that he will be; we long for the time when we will see him as he is (1 John 3:2) and know him as fully as he knows us (1 Corinthians 13:12).

In the liturgies of many churches, Holy Communion is celebrated explicitly as "a foretaste of the feast to come." The purpose of a foretaste is not to satisfy one's hunger but to make one long for the feast. It seems to me that the more often Christians take Communion, the more impatient they should become. I've been taking Communion almost weekly for about forty years now and my attitude is becoming "Enough with the appetizers! I want the feast!" Of course, we must be grateful for what we have. Grateful, but *not* satisfied! One purpose of Communion is to feed our impatience, simultaneously reminding us of our Lord's absence and allowing us to experience just enough of his presence to increase this longing in our souls.

The Christian life is marked by confident sadness and urgent anticipation. Recognizing the absence of Jesus allows us to face the reality of life in a way that avoids what Martin Luther called an unrealistic "theology of glory." Luther warned against an overly enthusiastic piety by which persons think that faith will enable them to rise above problems in life and enjoy a trouble-free existence. Such persons quote favorite Bible verses, including "We are more than conquerors through him who loved us" (Romans 8:37) and "I can do all things through him who strengthens me" (Philippians 4:13). Yes, but both of those verses were written by the apostle Paul who also had a thorn in his flesh that the Lord would not remove (2 Corinthians 12:7) and who often wrote of trials and tribulations that he suffered (2 Corinthians 11:24-25). Confident sadness allows us to live with faith that does not deny reality, faith that recognizes that life in this world is hard, and, indeed, not as it should be. We are not in glory yet. As one Christian rock star puts it, we still haven't found what we're looking for. Even at its best, this life is not as good as it gets. As citizens of heaven, we are but strangers and aliens on this earth (1 Peter 2:11), "only visiting this planet" (as yet another Christian rocker said). And we are in love with a bridegroom who has gone away.

# CHAPTER SEVEN

# Soon and Very Soon

I have said that Christians should be (somewhat) sad, and I have also indicated that they should be impatient. I speak of godly impatience, more akin to ardent enthusiasm than to that character flaw that leads to impetuous behavior or simple resignation. There is a patience that is a virtue to be pursued by all. "The patient in spirit are better than the proud in spirit," the Bible says (Ecclesiastes 7:8). And of course we are urged to "be patient in suffering" (Romans 12:12). In such cases, however, the word *patience* has the sense of *perseverance*. When the Bible says that we should "Be still before the Lord, and wait patiently for him" (Psalms 37:7; 40:1), it means that we should not despair or lose hope. Indeed, some versions of the Bible (including the NRSV) often translate the Greek word for patience (*hypomenē*) with such synonyms as *endurance* (Luke 21:19; Romans 5:3-4; 1 Timothy 6:11; James 1:3-4) or *steadfastness* (Romans 15:4-5; 2 Corinthians 6:4; 1 Thessalonians 1:3; 2 Thessalonians 1:4).

Well, certainly, we need to wait for the Lord with patient endurance (Luke 8:15; Revelation 1:9; 2:2, 3, 19; 3:10). Still, the Bible also encourages eager expectation of our Lord's return. We are told to "be on the watch," expecting Jesus to come back at any moment (Mark 13:34-35). This is not just a matter of "readiness," as preachers are inclined to portray it. Of course, we should be ready for the Lord to return, but we should also be waiting for that day with breathless anticipation. The Bible says that we should be literally *restless* (Mark 13:35). This constant restlessness is what I mean when I say that Christians should always be impatient. The biblical exhortations to patience were intended to restrain an enthusiasm that might otherwise turn into fanaticism. What sometimes bothers me about the current church is that, in mainline denominations at least, I don't see a lot of people who need to have their enthusiasm restrained. I want to arouse such enthusiasm and then, if it gets out of hand, we'll worry about tempering it with the necessary patience later.

The Bible warns us about false prophets who will lead people astray with misdirected announcements of the Lord's coming (Mark 13:21), but it also warns us about growing so lax that we no longer look for the coming of Jesus at all. The author of 2 Peter spoke well of our current generation when he wrote, "Scoffers will come . . . saying, 'Where is the promise of his coming? For ever since our ancestors died, all things continue as they were'" (2 Peter 3:3-4). In other words, people will think, "Many generations have come and gone without anything happening—why should it happen now?" Jesus told parables of judgment about people who get into trouble by playing the odds, servants who say, "My master is delayed," that is, he's been gone so long, what are the chances he'll return *tonight* (see Matthew 24:45-51; Luke 12:40-46).

But simply avoiding disgrace or punishment is hardly the point. Rather, when Christians cease to think of Jesus' return as something that could happen *immediately*, they miss out on one of the most joy-filled and life-giving aspects of Christian spirituality. Their faith may be doctrinally sound—but it is not likely to be *exciting*.

## What We Expect

Recognizing the absence of Jesus (a main theme from our last chapter) arouses urgent anticipation of his return. The Bible encourages this; indeed, I think it encourages us to expect Jesus to return soon, within our own lifetimes. Of course, it always allows that this might not happen. We might die, and we need not fear death, for God has that covered as well. But I think that death, if it comes, should take us by surprise. We do not expect to die—we expect Jesus to come for us. Such an expectation is not based on doctrine or intellectual speculation. It has nothing to do with prophecies being fulfilled over in Israel. It is more an expression of attitude or hope—a matter of the heart.

Prophecies in Israel? Okay, now I have touched on a controversial subject, and I guess it is only fair to say a bit more about it—but only a bit, or else we will never get back on track. Quite a few popular religious books have tried to establish that we are living in the final generation before Jesus' return by demonstrating that what they take to be prophecies of the end times are now being fulfilled somewhere in the world (especially in Israel). Virtually no critical Bible scholar takes these arguments seriously—and neither do I. Like most biblical scholars, I read Revelation as an example of a particular type of ancient literature (called "apocalyptic"), not as a collection of prophecies about modern times. Lots of apocalyptic books were written by Christians, Jews, and others, and though they may deal imaginatively and symbolically with the end times, they do not try to offer blueprints for determining when these end times will occur. Furthermore, I try to interpret Revelation (and all of the Bible) in light of its historical context; I try to discern what the book would have meant to *first-century* readers and on that basis discover its timeless meaning for all people. I think it is a mistake to read Revelation (or any other book of the Bible) as addressed to us today in a way that must assume it would have been meaningless to its original readers (and to virtually all readers ever since).

> Expecting Jesus to return soon is a matter of the heart, an expression of the poetic language of love that sustains our relationship with one who is both present with us and absent from us.

You may or may not agree with me on that matter, but my main point is that Christians may evince a heartfelt expectation of Jesus' imminent return *regardless* of what they think about the subject doctrinally. Personally, I think those who believe that Jesus will return soon on the basis of some doctrinal understanding of biblical prophecies (or of the book of Revelation) are wrong. That is, I think their doctrine is wrong. Ironically, I think they are nevertheless right to expect Jesus to return soon and I wish that, in this regard, we could all be like them.

At any rate, I do expect Jesus to return within my own lifetime, and I think the Bible encourages me to do so. The Bible promises that Jesus is coming soon (see the box on page 63). I admit that I don't know what "soon" means. One day with the Lord is like a thousand years (2 Peter 3:8). But *for me*, the only meaningful definition of "soon" is my lifetime. From a rational perspective, maybe it is just wishful thinking, but being a person of faith means more than just thinking about things from a rational perspective. Being a person of faith means loving Jesus Christ in a way that is certainly not just rational.

Here's how it works: I love Jesus, I miss him, and I long to be with him. When I read the Bible as God's living Word to me, and it says that Jesus is coming soon, that message touches the confident hope within me and turns it into an eager expectation of his return. I look for him to come "soon and very soon" (to quote a favorite Andraé Crouch song). Of course, if I sit down and reflect on the matter rationally, I might come to a different conclusion: people throughout history have experienced this expectation—why should it be fulfilled for me when it wasn't for them? But that's just it—I *don't* sit down and think about it rationally. Or, at least, I don't do so all the time.

Expecting Jesus to return soon is part of the *poetry* of faith (see above, pages 21–22). It is piety, not theology or doctrine. Poetry does not follow the rules of grammar, and piety does not always follow the rules of reason, but

---

**JESUS IS COMING SOON**

The apostle Paul says
- "Salvation is nearer to us now than when we became believers; the night is far gone, the day is near" (Romans 13:11-12).
- "The God of peace will shortly crush Satan under your feet" (Romans 16:20).
- "The appointed time has grown short" (1 Corinthians 7:29).
- "The Lord is near" (Philippians 4:5).

The first letter of Peter assures us
- "The end of all things is near" (1 Peter 4:7).

The author of Hebrews says
- "Yet in a very little while, the one who is coming will come and will not delay" (Hebrews 10:37).

James, the brother of our Lord, writes
- "Strengthen your hearts, for the coming of the Lord is near!" (James 5:8).

And in Revelation, Jesus himself says
- "See, I am coming soon" (Revelation 22:7).
- "See, I am coming soon" (Revelation 22:12).
- "Surely, I am coming soon" (Revelation 22:20).

---

both make sense in ways that transcend such rules. Expecting Jesus to return soon is a matter of the heart, an expression of the poetic language of love that sustains our relationship with one who is both present with us and absent from us.

## And Why Not?

When people ask me, "How can you expect Jesus to return in your own lifetime?" I sometimes want to turn that around and ask, "How can you *not* expect it?" If you love the Lord and want to be with him, then, when you read the Bible and it says that he is coming soon, why doesn't that promise go straight to your heart? Why doesn't it arouse within you an urgent expectation of fulfillment? Why don't you think these Scriptures apply to you?

I think I know why. At least, I think I know a few reasons why this might sometimes be the case. I have alluded to one of these already: we may want to avoid evincing an attitude that is sometimes embraced for reasons we would reject. Christians who refuse to *believe* that Jesus is coming soon as a matter of doctrine may find it hard to *expect* that Jesus is coming soon as an expression of their piety. The heart and the head are related, after all. In particular, people who once believed "that stuff" in a naïve way may think that I am suggesting they return to a stage of faith that they have come to regard as simplistic. But I present this as one more instance of the "second naïveté": intellectual speculation gives way to intuitive expectation (see page 12). Yes, it may have been naïve to believe Jesus was coming soon for the reasons we once did (bad exegesis, opportunistic preaching, dispensational theology, and so on). Yes, it might also be naïve to expect him to return soon even now, for completely different reasons (as a hope of the heart, not as a doctrinal proposition). Still, the second naïveté is not like the first. It is grounded in humility, not ignorance, and it gives expression to the sort of innocence that the Bible seeks to instill in us.

Another reason we might resist expecting Jesus to return soon is that we don't want to give up on this world, but rather concentrate on making it a better place to live. Such a commitment is commendable, but seems to build upon a misguided (oft-stated) assumption that those who expect Jesus to return soon are lulled into passivity, waiting for heaven rather than working for the present world's improvement. My experience is that this is seldom the case—Christians who are looking for their Lord to come busy themselves all the more doing those things that he would want them to do. So there is an apocryphal tale of Martin Luther being asked what he would do *today* if he knew Jesus would return *tomorrow*. Supposedly, he replied, "Plant a tree" (or in some versions of the story, "Hoe my garden"). The point is that whenever our Lord comes, we want him to find us doing God's will: caring for this planet and serving our neighbor. Humans are good at paradox. We all know how to "prepare for the worst while hoping for the best." So, too, we can use our wits to live in ways that will benefit future generations while simultaneously hoping in our hearts for the great miracle that will render such efforts superfluous.

This heartfelt expectation of Jesus' return has suffered from other quarters as well. Modern science has had its say, such that the images the Bible uses do not always appeal to those who have been conditioned to think about the world in other categories. The sky splitting open? Angels descending? Trumpets blowing? And horses—white, red, black, and pale green—a rainbow posse of horses in the sky (see Revelation 6:1-8)? Such language depicts the end times as something surreal, something that just seems much less likely than mushroom clouds and fallout haze. But the purpose of images is to stimulate the imagination. When I *imagine* the return of Jesus, in my mind, the scenario always involves the images from the Bible. In my mind, I see horses and angels. At one level, I don't think that it will really be like that. To the extent that I understand what modern science teaches about our universe, I accept and believe that the scientific perspective is correct. The sky is only air—it cannot split. And if there really are such spiritual beings as angels (this I do believe), why would they need horses? Or trumpets? But none of this stops me from imagining a world that lies beyond the realm of scientific exploration. I do so without apology, and yet I do not believe that this spiritual realm is "only imaginary." It is our *apprehension* of the world that is imaginary (or symbolic or mythological), for we "see through a glass, darkly" (1 Corinthians 13:12 KJV) and are not able to comprehend in literal terms those dimensions of reality that are not accessible to our senses. So I not only expect Jesus to return, but I *imagine* this return to involve horses and angels and trumpets and all sorts of other accoutrements that, when the time comes, will probably turn out to have been symbolic or mythological depictions of things that my poor mind was not able to conceive. I think it is very important for Christians to be able to think rationally, intellectually, and scientifically about the world in which they live, but it is also very important that such thought processes not destroy their powers of imagination. The first theology professor I ever had (as a college freshman) told me, "Don't commit intellectual suicide for the sake of your faith." That was an important lesson. I would now add a corollary: don't commit spiritual suicide for the sake of your intellect. And spiritual truth is often conveyed with imagery that transcends intellectual understanding.

Finally, I'm sorry to say that Bible scholars have also played a significant role in depriving everyday Christians of the heartfelt expectation of their Lord's return. The effect of much well-intentioned biblical scholarship has been to *historicize* the Scriptures so that they speak primarily to another setting, addressed to a situation long ago and far away. There is need for historical understanding of Scripture, but the Bible is also a living Word through which God speaks to people today. I indicated the way it is supposed to work in the paragraph on Revelation above. New Testament scholars are supposed to discern what the biblical writer meant to say to readers in the first century, and by doing this they are supposed to discover what the timeless meaning of the biblical writing might be for people in our own day. Most of the time, I think it does work that way—but not always. Sometimes, discerning the meaning of a biblical passage for its original audience seems to blunt the text for application in any other setting. This seems to have happened with regard to biblical promises that the Lord is coming soon. Bible scholars often don't know what to do with those promises except to acknowledge that, obviously, the Lord did *not* come soon. So the writers must have been mistaken or meant something different that we just don't understand.

I think it is very important for Christians to be able to think rationally, intellectually, and scientifically about the world in which they live, but it is also very important that such thought processes not destroy their powers of imagination.

Here's what I think: when James, the brother of our Lord, wrote that "the coming of the Lord is near" (James 5:8), he wanted all the people in the first century who read his letter to expect Jesus to return soon. It was a declaration of his heart, an encouragement to emotional hope rather than an intellectual declaration of doctrine—and his readers received it as such. We may note, for instance, that Christian leaders in the first few centuries after the letter was written were not troubled by the thought that maybe James had made a mistake and issued false promises. No one said, "Wait. This can't be Scripture. He said that the coming of the Lord was near and it wasn't." No, when they read James 5:8, they read the verse as addressed to *them* and were

66

excited by this testimony of Scripture that (still) promised the Lord would come soon. That, I think, is exactly the way James would have wanted his letter to be read. The timeless meaning of the text is found in the *effect* that it is intended to have on its readers: anyone, anywhere, at any time who reads this letter is to be encouraged with the words, "The coming of the Lord is near." The same may be said for the other passages cited on page 63. I suspect that most of the New Testament authors hoped to instill in their readers an urgent anticipation of Jesus' imminent return, not as a matter of academic dogma but as an emotional attitude of faith, an expression of heartfelt hope. We yield to the intent of Scripture by allowing this goal to be fulfilled in us.

All I can say is, it works for me. It didn't before, but now it does. A long time ago, when I was a teenaged Jesus freak, I believed that Jesus would return soon. It was exciting to believe that and it filled my life with hope and joy. I believed it for all sorts of misguided doctrinal reasons that I would renounce today. For a while, once I learned how to understand the Bible better and I became more intellectually respectable (less naïve), that wonderful expectation just vanished away. And then, it came back. I don't know how. I don't know why. I just read my Bible, and when it said, "The Lord is coming soon!" I felt that word was not just addressed to people in some other time and place, but that it was God's promise to me as well. It was as though I had traveled *through* something and come out the other side, and the whole Jesus freak thing came back in all its freaky glory.

## Checking the Skies

In my church, there is a point in the liturgical, eucharistic service where the whole congregation says, "Amen! Come, Lord Jesus!" Nowadays, I always look when we say that. I glance out the windows and up at the ceiling. I look to see if maybe he will come, right then, at that moment. I figure, what's the point of praying for it if you don't expect it to happen, if you don't at least allow that it *might*?

I love cloudy days now. The Bible says that Jesus is coming with the clouds (Mark 13:26). I figure, the more clouds there are, the better the chances that today's the day. Another theology professor rebuked me for such simplicity: "It's not cloudy all over the world," he said. "How do you know Jesus will return right *here*? Maybe he'll come back somewhere else when there are no clouds over our heads. Maybe he'll come back on the other side of the globe, and you won't even see it."

My response: "People who are in love don't think about things like that."

Another professor said, "You know the apostle Paul believed Jesus was going to return during his lifetime—and *he* was wrong!"

My response: (1) Would that all my faults could be compared to those of the apostle; (2) Paul did not *believe* Jesus was going to return during his lifetime: he *expected* Jesus to return during his lifetime; and, (3) He was not wrong; he was right—he was right to expect this.

I feel like I've covered this, but let's say it one more time. It is clear from Paul's letters that he expects Christ to return while some of his readers (which would include us) are still alive (1 Corinthians 15:51-52; 1 Thessalonians 4:15). He urges his readers (including us) to expect this as well. But in all those letters Paul never indicates that he has worked out some kind of a timetable for predicting the parousia (that is, the Second Coming), or that he thinks Jesus will return soon because of prophecies that he sees being fulfilled. He never presents the belief that "Jesus will return by such-and-such a date" as a doctrinal teaching to be apprehended intellectually—a view that we would now have to regard as a mistake. Rather, Paul just seems to have loved Jesus so much that he looked every day for his Lord to come, waiting, hoping, and, yes, expecting it to happen. And when Paul laid his head on the chopping block on that fateful day a scant three decades after his Lord's own execution, I do not think that his last thoughts on this earth were, "Well, I guess I was wrong." If anything, I suspect he was checking the sky for clouds and expecting to hear trumpets. That didn't happen, but when death came to the apostle Paul, I think it came as a surprise. He had, of course, reckoned with the possibility, prepared himself mentally and emotionally as he sat in prison awaiting his fate (Philippians 1:20-21; compare Romans 14:8). Still, there is always a sense in which Christians do not expect to die. If we do die, God has that covered too. But death is not our destiny, and what we really expect is for our Lord Jesus to come for us soon.

> Death is not our destiny, and what we really expect is for our Lord Jesus to come for us soon.

*The primitive church thought more about the Second Coming of Jesus Christ than about death or about heaven. The early Christians were not looking for a cleft in the ground called a grave but for a cleavage in the sky called Glory. They were watching not for the undertaker but for the uppertaker.*

Alexander MacLaren

*I hope the day is near at hand when the advent of our great God will appear, for all things everywhere are boiling, burning, moving, falling, sinking, groaning.*

Martin Luther

*We are not in a post-war generation, but a pre-peace generation. Jesus is coming.*

Corrie ten Boom, holocaust survivor

# CHAPTER EIGHT

# A Flicker in Time

Years ago, when I was a young parish pastor, I had the occasion to hold the hand of a dying woman once a week for two years. I was young; she was old. She was sick and bedfast. I visited her once a week to bring her Communion and say a prayer. Everyone knew she was dying, but she was like that for two years—and then she finally did die.

Her name was Sara, and I used to read the church newsletter to her. Sometimes it was a little embarrassing, because it contained hints of problems that churches often have. A couple of families wanted to leave our church because they didn't like the new hymnal. The church council was trying to decide what to do about inactive members. The annual meeting erupted in controversy over a proposed remodeling project. After reading Sara the newsletter, I would always want to read her the twenty-third psalm, or the Beatitudes, or something else that I thought might be more uplifting.

One time, she took my hand and said, "Pastor, I want you to tell everyone something for me." What is it? "Tell them, if they've got their health, they've got *nothing* to complain about."

That stuck with me as a young pastor and as a young human being. There are a lot of bad things in this world, but I think that sickness has got to be among the worst. It causes so much suffering—so much pain and distress for the one who is ill, and sometimes, even more pain and distress for those who care about them.

I have never been seriously sick like that myself, but one time I did have a twenty-four-hour virus that had me rethinking my opposition to euthanasia. It was so horrible, I just wanted to die. But the odd thing was, once I got better, I couldn't really remember what it felt like to be sick. I remembered it was awful, but the feeling itself was just gone. I laugh about it now—that little flicker in time when I felt so bad. I suspect that someday we will remember this life that way. We will remember that life in this world had pain and suffering—but *pain* and *suffering* will be such foreign concepts, we won't even be able to remember what they were. This whole life—a flicker in time.

## No Good Reason Why

Jesus used a different metaphor to speak of suffering: "When a woman is in labor, she has pain, because her hour has come. But when her child is born, she no longer remembers the anguish because of the joy of having brought a human being into the world" (John 16:21). Childbirth may provide a better analogy for understanding our present plight than "a day with the flu," because it suggests that the suffering we experience is purposeful—it produces something worthwhile; indeed, it produces life. Sometimes, that seems to be the case. I would like to think that all of our pains and trials serve some kind of noble purpose, if only in a mysterious way that we do not always understand. The Bible maintains that suffering can have a refining effect (1 Peter 1:7), and even secular wisdom holds that "whatever doesn't kill you can make you stronger." This view is expressed with special optimism in the letter of James: "Whenever you face trials of any kind, consider it nothing but joy, because you know that the testing of your faith produces endurance" (James 1:2).

Well, that's a nice thought—and I'm sure it's *true* (being in the Bible and all)—but, frankly, I don't always *see* that it's true. I see all kinds of suffering and trials in this world that don't seem to accomplish any good for anyone at all. If it's all part of some great divine plan, then I must be out of the loop, and I'm left with a lot of unanswered questions. It doesn't help—at least, it doesn't help me—to be told that "everything happens for a reason."

What I *think* is (1) there are different kinds of suffering in this world, and (2) it is simplistic to take Bible verses that speak of one kind and apply them to every kind. There is suffering that comes to us as a consequence of our own bad judgment or misdeeds—and sometimes this kind of suffering serves the purpose of making us wiser or better behaved. Life is also filled with difficulties and challenges that are not our fault but that still might build character and bolster our faith. "If I'd never had a problem," croons gospel singer Andraé Crouch, "I wouldn't know that God could solve them." The apostle Paul also finds value in pain: "Suffering produces endurance, and endurance produces character, and character produces hope" (Romans 5:3-4) (28)

But then there is suffering that appears to serve no good purpose whatsoever. A maternity ward filled with newborn babies is wiped out by a hurricane or an earthquake. Does this happen "for a reason"? Yes, and the reason is this: the world is out of control, and God's will is no longer being done. Sometimes the Bible allows that it is the devil and not God who calls the shots in this life. "The whole world lies under the power of the evil one," the Bible says (1 John 5:19; see also Luke 4:6; John 14:30; 2 Corinthians 4:4; Ephesians 6:12). Of course, the Bible also says that Satan has been bound, so his power is limited, but perhaps not *as* limited as we would like. Martin Luther said that God has put the devil on a leash—and Lutherans have been saying ever since that the leash appears to be a long one.

For many, the inexplicable presence of suffering in this world is an obstacle to faith. The motion picture *The Hiding Place* depicts a conversation that Holocaust survivor Corrie ten Boom had with another prisoner while imprisoned in a concentration camp. "If God wants to help us, but can't, then God is not powerful," the prisoner reasons. "And if God *can* help us, but won't, then God does not care." It is a thought-provoking observation, yet ten Boom and many other prisoners did come out of those camps with their faith in a caring and powerful God intact. Why?

I defer to a remark I heard a hospital chaplain make. A baby had been born with a malignant tumor in his brain. He had no chance of survival, and he was in pain. The child had been born into this world to suffer for a few days and then die. A doctor met the chaplain in a private room where this child lay crying in his bed and said abruptly, "I think God has to be pretty cruel to allow something like this to happen." Why would a doctor make such a comment (to a chaplain)? Obviously, he was frustrated by the limits of medical science to bring help in such a situation, and perhaps he wanted to test the theological expert to see if *his* field had anything to offer. He certainly wanted a response, and when the chaplain said nothing, he pressed for one: "Huh? Chaplain? What do *you* think?" And then the chaplain replied, "I guess if this were all the evidence I had to go on, I would have to agree with you."

The wisdom of that response lies in its reluctance to claim more than can be known. Chaplains, pastors, and theologians do not ultimately know why suffering is so prominent a part of human existence. We have a few ideas, but no proposal that answers all the questions. We do *not* believe that it's just because Adam and Eve ate that apple (or pomegranate or whatever it was). Nor do we believe that everything bad can be attributed to the work of the devil (who was, at any rate, created by God, and often has human assistants). Philosophers muse about the inevitable consequences of "free will" and of an "open universe," but few people find those arguments completely persuasive, much less comforting. No one really knows why a powerful and loving God allows people (or even animals) to suffer; still there *is* more to life than suffering. Agnostics and skeptics also face an overwhelming problem: How do you explain beauty or pleasure or compassion or joy? Whence comes *love*— even sacrificial love that goes against every evolutionary urge for survival? Why is there *life*—and why is life often so good? Suffering is real, but it's not all the evidence we have to go on.

The claim of Christian Scripture is that there is a problem, and it will be fixed. We don't claim to understand fully just what the problem is, and we don't claim that, ultimately, we will be the ones to fix it. Of course, we try to understand, and we do what we can to make things better, but in the final analysis our efforts amount to tinkering. We've been at such tinkering for a long time, and we've gotten pretty good at it. We've made incredible advances that improve the lives of millions of people, but eventually creation itself is going to have to be transformed, and that is a job for the Creator.

> Things are not the way they should be, but God will fix them. So why doesn't God fix everything *immediately*?

The fact is, many bad things happen to good people simply because the universe itself is broken and needs repair. Such suffering is not God's will. It is not redemptive, and it is not even necessary. It is just bad. It's horrible. And the Bible really has only one thing to say about such suffering: it will end.

Things are not the way they should be, but God will fix them. So why doesn't God fix everything *immediately*? Well, that's the real mystery. If we ask *that* question, we may be left staring into an empty cosmos that refuses to answer us. Or, like Job, we may discover that we have aroused the anger of a deity who does not appreciate being called on the carpet by tiny mortals who think they should be in charge of setting such timetables (Job 40–41).

"So much pain and no good reason why," sings Amy Grant. "And all that I can say is somewhere down the road there will be answers." There's a lot we don't know, but what we *do* know is that suffering will end, and that, when it does, we will hardly even remember what it was like. Our difficult lives are but a flicker in time, less than a flicker in eternity. "After you have suffered for a little while," the first letter of Peter promises, "the God of all grace, who has called you to his eternal glory in Christ, will himself restore, support, strengthen, and establish you" (1 Peter 5:10). Whatever we suffer is only "for a little while," and then it will end.

---

### WHAT GOD HAS PREPARED FOR US

No More Suffering

> The sufferings of this present time are not worth comparing with the glory about to be revealed to us.
>
> Romans 8:18

Heaven and Earth Made New

> We wait for new heavens and a new earth, where righteousness is at home.
>
> 2 Peter 3:13

And We, Also, Made New

> We will be changed. For this perishable body must put on imperishability, and this mortal body must put on immortality.
>
> 1 Corinthians 15:52-53

We Will Know All Things

> Now I know only in part; then I will know fully, even as I have been fully known.
>
> 1 Corinthians 13:12

We Will Be Like Christ

> When he is revealed, we will be like him, for we will see him as he is.
>
> 1 John 3:2

Still, More (Beyond What We Can Imagine)

> What no eye has seen, nor ear heard, nor the human heart conceived . . . God has prepared for those who love him.
>
> 1 Corinthians 2:9, cf. Isaiah 64:4

Set in place

---

## The Glory to Be Revealed

We wait with confident hope for life to be the way it is supposed to be. But for now we live in a treacherous world, captured well in these verses of a Jonathan Rundman song ("Deadly Life"):

> We didn't starve or thirst to death or fall to some disease
> We weren't lost or all alone or left outside to freeze
> There was no freeway accident or collapse of the sun
> We didn't die the victim of some punk kid with a gun
> There was no right wing terrorist or killer flash flood
> We weren't sent to fight no war, we got no tainted blood
> We weren't in the path of some drunk man at the wheel
> The day was rough but we got through, so every night we kneel
> There's a holy miracle every single night
> When we lie down in our beds and turn out all the lights
> We breathed ourselves another day, we beat all the odds
> We survived this deadly life and gave it back to God.

That's what we do in this life—we thank God for mere *survival*. And if we have our *health* we really have nothing worth complaining about. But life is meant to be so much more—and it will be! "The sufferings of this present time are not worth comparing with the glory about to be revealed to us," Paul says (Romans 8:18).

Imagine a world with no sickness. Nobody gets the flu. Nobody gets cancer. No one has AIDS. And more: the Bible says no hunger, no war, no poverty, no greed or injustice. More than that: "And God . . . will wipe every tear from their eyes" (Revelation 21:4). No more loneliness. No more broken hearts. "Death will be no more," the Bible continues (Revelation 21:4). "Mourning and crying and pain will be no more." No more car accidents and late night phone calls. No child will ever have to bury his or her parent—and no parent will ever again have to bury his or her child.

What Paul calls "the glory to be revealed" is not just a world where suffering can be avoided or minimized. "Creation itself will be set free from its bondage to decay," Paul writes (Romans 8:21). The very universe will be transformed and things will be the way they should be. Near the end of the book of Revelation, we are promised that there will be "a new heaven and a new earth; for the first heaven and the first earth had passed away" (Revelation 21:1).

Have you ever had a product under warranty that kept breaking? I had one once, an item from an electronics store. It was a "lemon," I guess. The warranty said they would fix it or replace it free. Guess which they did? They fixed it—over and over again. It got a bit frustrating. Every time I'd haul the thing in, they'd fix it, but I knew it was just going to break again. After a while, I figured they knew this, too, but they just weren't going to cough up and replace this piece of junk with a new item that wouldn't need fixing in the first place. I know the analogy is flawed, but at times I feel like this universe is beyond repair. It's basically a good world we live in, but no matter how much we (with God's help) try to fix it up, something else always seems to go wrong. And then *here*—in the fine print at the end of the Bible—God seems to say, If it can't be fixed I'll give you a new one—free! And unlike any warranty I've ever had, this one is not voided by negligence or abuse. The promise of a new world—a new heaven and a new earth—holds even if what's wrong with the old one turns out to be our fault. That sounds like a good deal to me.

> The promise of a new world— a new heaven and a new earth—holds even if what's wrong with the old one turns out to be our fault.

So, what exactly does this mean? What will life be like in this "new heaven and new earth"? We usually conceive of the "glory to be revealed" in terms of deletion—a world that lacks all the bad things we experience in this life. Such is the finitude of our minds, but the Bible assures us that the new *positive* attributes of our glorious future will far outweigh a simple elimination of negatives. The reality lies beyond our powers of comprehension, but we are offered a few tantalizing hints.

We will have new bodies, Paul tells us (1 Corinthians 15:52-53). We won't just be ghosts, some sort of intelligent vapor floating about in a celestial stew. We will have *bodies*—much more glorious and beautiful bodies than we had in this life. My body isn't much—it never was too impressive even at its best, and these days it keeps breaking down. Of course, I try to thank God for what I've got, but I also look forward to trading up.

We will know everything, even as we have been fully known. "Now I know only in part," Paul says, in what amounts to a colossal understatement (1 Corinthians 13:12). We "see in a mirror, dimly," an optimistic appraisal of our abilities at best. But someday, all mysteries will be revealed, and we will know God as well as God knows us.

There is more at stake here than the mere satisfaction of curiosity. The Bible indicates that God's glory contains transforming power. When we behold the glory of Jesus Christ, we are changed into his likeness. Thus, Paul says that already in this life, to the limited extent that we can behold the glory of the Lord, we are "being transformed into the same image from one degree of glory to another" (2 Corinthians 3:18). But, someone will argue, that would mean that if we were able to see Jesus as he truly is we might become like him—and that cannot be possible. Actually, that *is* possible and is exactly what is going to happen. The Bible says, "when he is revealed, we will be like him, for we will see him as he is" (1 John 3:2). Thus St. Athanasius could maintain, "He was made human that we might be made divine" (*On the Incarnation of the Word of God,* 54). Someday, we will share Christ's glory— we will be like him.

The promises of God are better than anything we might have imagined. It is one thing to live in a world without suffering. It is better yet to live in a paradise filled with pleasure. People often imagine the world to come as being like the Garden of Eden. That's not too far off, I suppose, but the Bible says it will be even better than that. This time, we will be allowed to eat from that forbidden Tree of Life (Revelation 2:14), and even the serpents will be harmless (Isaiah 11:8). But lest we think that living in a perfect world is the best God has for us, the Bible promises still more: we ourselves will be perfected. Come to think of it, life in a perfect world might be kind of embarrassing for imperfect people—we would sort of stand out, and I guess the world would not actually be perfect for anyone who knew us. So God has that covered, too: we will be "holy and blameless and irreproachable" (Colossians 1:22; Ephesians 1:4). I suppose this means that even my little problem with snoring will be fixed, a minor matter, but one that has been known to render me reproachable in this current life.

Perfect people living in a perfect world—that's it! Or, actually, that's not it, because the Bible says there is even more that we cannot fathom. Things that no one has ever seen or heard or even thought about—what has never entered into the imagination of any human being—*that,* the Bible says, is what God has prepared for those who love God (2 Corinthians 2:9).

## Knowing How It Ends

I boarded a subway one time and sat near an odd-looking young man who was holding a very large Bible. He was dressed in leather, like some kind of street punk, and he was grinning from ear to ear. He reminded me of myself when I was a teenaged Jesus freak (except for the leather—we wore tie-dye). One does not often see street punks holding very large books, much less Bibles, on the subway, so I could not help but intrude. I leaned over and asked him, "Have you read that book?" He looked at me and grinned. Then he said, "Not all of it, but I took a look at the ending and . . . *we win!*" That is perhaps the best interpretation of Revelation I have ever heard. Revelation is a very complicated book, but in the final analysis there's not a lot more to it than that: when all is said and done, we will find our happy ending—and it will never end.

> When all is said and done, we will find our happy ending— and it will never end.

This is our destiny, what God prepared for us before the foundation of the world (Matthew 25:34). This is the hope for which we wait. Waiting can be hard, of course. But the Bible calls us again and again to wait for the Lord (Psalm 27:14). The Bible says that "those who wait for the Lord shall renew their strength, they shall mount up with wings like eagles, they shall run and not be weary, they shall walk and not faint" (Isaiah 40:31). And again, it says, "If we hope for what we do not see, we wait for it with patience" (Romans 8:25). And the brother of our Lord says this:

> Be, patient, therefore, beloved, until the coming of the Lord. The farmer waits for the precious crop from the earth, being patient with it until it receives the early and the late rains. You also must be patient. Strengthen your hearts, for the coming of the Lord is near. (James 5:7-8)

Ah, yes, patience. It's a good thing—we must pray for it. But, I notice that this encouragement to patience is founded on the proposition that "the coming of the Lord is near." We are not expected simply to dig in for the long haul, assuming that the Lord might not come back for centuries. We are to be patient for "a very little while" (Hebrews 10:37) in the expectation that the Lord is coming soon.

In a previous chapter I indicated what I think it "feels like" to be a Christian: I said that sometimes "it feels like being in love with someone who has gone away" (page 55). Yes, sometimes that's right, but what it *should* feel like when our faith and spirituality are at their best is "being in love with someone who is about to return." Imagine a young woman whose husband is sent overseas for a couple of years. Now he's coming back. She's at the terminal, *waiting*, scanning the faces of every new group of disembarking passengers. How do you think she feels? *That's* what it feels like to be a Christian. That's what it should feel like, when we catch the vision that Scripture offers us and allow the biblical promises to affect our hearts.

Perhaps you are wondering if we have strayed from the official subject of this book—loving Jesus in a complicated world. No, we are just reflecting on the "complicated" part, and we shall continue to do so (in different ways) for a couple more chapters. Growth in spirituality, and in *piety*, can be facilitated by a proper understanding of our current situation. So, if we want to love Jesus deeply and meaningfully, we must realize both how he is present with us and how he is absent from us. And if we want our love for Jesus to thrive amidst the threats and trials of this deadly life, we must become fully aware of both the reality of suffering and the power of hope. We wait on the Lord with strained patience and restrained enthusiasm. We live on the brink of something that is always "about to happen." We are promised a paradise, a kingdom of heaven that seems to be always "at hand" but never quite *here*. That is the character of Christian life in this present world.

For Christians, all suffering is a product of the wait. Thus, all suffering is temporary (just a flicker in time), and all suffering is made bearable by hope. The biblical concept of *hope* is so much more powerful than what is conveyed by our English word. We often use the word *hope* to express a mere wish. When we say that we hope something will happen, we mean that we would like for it to happen, though it might or might not. But the Bible speaks of a hope that "does not disappoint us" (Romans 5:5), a hope grounded in God's promises. Through Scripture and through the revelation of God in Jesus Christ, we know certain things about the future, and we know these things *for certain*. We are going to live forever in a glorious paradise where there is no pain or grief, in constant fellowship with those we love. This is the hope that God guarantees will not disappoint us. This is our destiny, the reality for which we wait.

— until we know God, and learn to hope the promised blessings in Christ; hope is only a human dream with no possibility. — JWC

# CHAPTER NINE

# Already and Not Yet

Jesus talked more about "the kingdom of God" than he did about anything else. He said that people should seek God's kingdom (Matthew 6:33) and pray regularly for it to come (Matthew 6:10). He told numerous parables about the kingdom and sometimes referred to what he called the "secrets" or "mysteries" of God's kingdom (Matthew 13:11). Above all, he announced that the kingdom of God had "come near" and insisted that this proclamation was good news that should inspire people to repent and believe the gospel (Mark 1:15).

This prolific theme in the teaching of Jesus is often understood differently at a popular level than it is by persons who have studied the Bible professionally. Most scholars agree on certain basic points regarding this theme that, for some reason, have not become widely known among average Bible readers.

The first point on which most scholars agree is that the phrase *kingdom of God* is itself inadequate. The Greek phrase is *basileia tou theou*, and it does not really mean "kingdom of God" in the sense that most people take those words. We will spend only a short time on these potentially boring matters of linguistics. The word *basileia* in Greek is an action noun (what is called a "cognate noun"). It is formed on the same root as a verb (*basileuō*) and, thus, it is a noun that expresses action. We have action nouns in English too: the word *baptism* refers to an action by which someone baptizes someone else, and the word *sin* refers to some act or activity of sinning. The English word *kingdom*, however, is not an action noun ("to kingdom" is not a verb), and it usually refers to a place, not an activity. The Greek word that *kingdom* is supposed to translate (*basileia*) rarely refers to a place, but to *the activity of someone ruling*. Thus, New Testament scholars are virtually unanimous in saying that the phrase *basileia tou theou* would be better translated with some expression that conveys this idea of action: "rule of God" or "reign of God" are frequent suggestions.

Why does this matter? Many people, I think, believe that the phrase "kingdom of God" in their English Bibles refers to a location—a place where God and angels live and where they themselves hope to go after they die. They read all the different Bible verses in light of this:

*God's power, authority, Reign takes place continually through those who trust and one leading God. JWC.*

- When Jesus says that we should seek first the kingdom of God (Matthew 6:33), they assume this means that our first priority in life should be making sure we will go to heaven and live with God when we die.
- When Jesus says it is harder for a rich person to enter the kingdom of God than for a camel to pass through the eye of a needle (Mark 10:25), they think this means it is all but impossible for rich people to go to heaven and live with God when they die.
- When Jesus says that no one can see the kingdom of God without being born again (John 3:3), they assume this means that people must get "born again" in this life in order to go to heaven and live with God when they die.

Such interpretations are not so much wrong as they are limited. Jesus is not talking *primarily* about a place where God lives, or where people might go after death. He is talking about a phenomenon that is not bound by space or time, the phenomenon of *God ruling people's lives*. What Jesus means in the above passages might be worded like this:

- Above all, we should seek to let God rule our lives.
- It is all but impossible for God to rule the life of a rich person.
- One's life cannot be ruled by God unless one is born again.

I hasten to add that such comments do not exhaust the meaning of Jesus' provocative remarks. Most commentators would grant that sayings like these do have some implications for life with God beyond death. The point, rather, is that the "kingdom of God" is not simply a place that can be located spatially ("in heaven") or temporally ("in the future"). It is a reality that exists wherever and whenever God rules the lives of God's people.

One easy way to remember this is by recalling these lines from the Lord's Prayer:

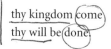

> thy kingdom come
> thy will be done

These lines are an example of synonymous parallelism, a poetic device by which one says the same thing twice in slightly different words. The device is common in the psalms; here is an example from Psalm 103:

> Bless the Lord, O my soul,
> and all that is within me,
> bless his holy name.

The three lines make exactly the same point, in different words. This is also true for the two lines from the Lord's Prayer: God's kingdom comes whenever God's will is done, because God can be said to rule whenever what God wants to happen takes place. Thus, when we pray, "thy kingdom come, thy will be done," we are asking for the same thing twice: we are asking God to rule our lives.

What, then, did Jesus mean when he came into Galilee and announced, "The time is fulfilled, and the kingdom of God has come near" (Mark 1:15)? *What* time had been fulfilled? The time for God's will to be done. What Jesus meant was this: "It is finally time for what God wants to happen to take place—God is ready to start ruling people's lives!" Jesus said that this announcement was "good news," and he hoped everyone who heard it would be inspired to "repent and believe."

## Present and Future

Jesus talked about God's rule as a present reality, insisting that something new and unprecedented was at hand. God had always ruled the nation of Israel, protecting and guiding them through prophets, priests, and political leaders.

God had always heard people's prayers and accepted their sacrifices. But now, Jesus claimed, God's rule had "come near" in a way that it never had before.

This happened in Jesus' own ministry. The claim of the Bible is that Jesus was able to do the things he did and to say the things he said because God's rule was being established in an unprecedented way. For example, Jesus told the religious leaders of his day, "If it is by the Spirit of God that I cast out demons, then the kingdom of God has come to you" (Matthew 12:28). In essence, he was saying, "If it is by God's power that I am liberating people from evil, then you should take this as proof that God is willing and able to rule people's lives."

What was true of Jesus' exorcisms would also be true of his other miracles and healings—opening the eyes of the blind, cleansing lepers, and raising people from the dead. These were all signs that God was in charge and interested in human affairs. Likewise, Jesus' habit of dining with outcasts was a sign of the *scope* of God's rule. God cares not only for the noble, the wise, and the powerful, but also (indeed, especially) for the dishonored, the foolish, and the weak. The "good news" Jesus proclaimed was, "We have a powerful God who cares about us—*all* of us—and who is willing and able to rule our lives."

Perhaps the most telling passage in Scripture regarding the kingdom of God as a present reality is this one:

> Once Jesus was asked by the Pharisees when the kingdom of God was coming, and he answered, "The kingdom of God is not coming with things that can be observed; nor will they say, 'Look, here it is!' or 'There it is!' For, in fact, the kingdom of God is among you." (Luke 17:20-21)

The point here seems to be, "Don't *wait* for the kingdom—*experience* it!" I remember what John Lennon said (a couple of months before he died): "Life is what happens to you while you're busy making other plans." The kingdom (that is, the rule or reign of God) is already here, and people who associate it only with heaven or with life after death risk missing out on what is available here and now.

But Jesus also spoke of God's rule as a *future* reality. He told his disciples to pray for the rule of God to come (Matthew 6:10). He said that when the rule of God is established, the poor will be blessed, the hungry will be filled, and those who weep will laugh (Luke 6:20-21). When God rules, people will come from all around to enjoy table fellowship with such notables as Abraham, Isaac, and Jacob (Matthew 8:11).

Is this a contradiction? Another one of those biblical paradoxes? Most scholars insist that the Bible describes God's rule as *both* a present and a future reality, or, to use their favorite phrase, as a phenomenon that is both "already and not yet." Discerning the difference between the Already and the Not Yet is at the core of biblical theology. This book, I have promised, is less concerned with theology than with piety. We do not need to understand everything to appreciate the implications of biblical truth for loving Jesus in a complicated world. Still, we are pressing now for a better understanding of one basic point that will be helpful in making sense of our spiritual journeys.

> Discerning the difference between the Already and the Not Yet is at the core of biblical theology.

The Bible uses different pictures for conveying this notion of the Already and the Not Yet. One is particularly colorful, another philosophical. We'll take the colorful one first.

---

THE REIGN OF GOD:

MORE SCRIPTURE TEXTS REGARDING GOD'S KINGDOM

When is the kingdom *present*? When is it *future*? When is it both?

- "The kingdom of God is as if someone would scatter seed on the ground, and would sleep and rise night and day, and the seed would sprout and grow, he does not know how" (Mark 4:26-27).

- "There are some standing here who will not taste death until they see that the kingdom of God has come with power" (Mark 9:1).

- "It is better for you to enter the kingdom of God with one eye than to have two eyes and to be thrown into hell" (Mark 9:47).

- "Let the little children come to me; do not stop them; for it is to such as these that the kingdom of God belongs" (Mark 10:14).

- "Whoever does not receive the kingdom of God as a little child will never enter it" (Mark 10:15).

- "I will never again drink of the fruit of the vine until that day when I drink it new in the kingdom of God" (Mark 14:25).

---

> - "The kingdom of God is not food and drink but righteousness and peace and joy in the Holy Spirit" (Romans 14:17).
>
> - "The kingdom of God depends not on talk but on power" (1 Corinthians 4:20).
>
> - "Flesh and blood cannot inherit the kingdom of God" (1 Corinthians 15:50).
>
> See also the passages discussed in this chapter: Matthew 6:10, 33; 8:11; 12:28; Mark 1:15; 10:25; Luke 6:20-21; 17:20-21; John 3:3.

# The Imprisoned Tyrant

Sometimes the Bible indicates that the real problem with this world is that it is ruled by the devil (see above on pages 71–72). God created the universe, but the devil mutinied and has apparently chosen our sphere of existence as his base of operations. But, the Bible continues, God has a two-step plan for dealing with this problem. First, the devil is to be bound—tied up or imprisoned. Then, at the end of the world, the devil will be thrown into a lake of fire to be destroyed forever (Matthew 25:41; Revelation 2:10). According to Jesus, the first step has already been taken: the devil is now God's captive (Matthew 12:29), awaiting his inevitable punishment.

To modernize the idiom we might say that the devil is on death row. He has already been arrested, tried, convicted, and sentenced. Still, like some convicted mafioso, he tries to run things from his prison cell, and he often succeeds. His influence has not been squelched, for many still fear him and can be intimidated into doing his bidding. Thus, evil persists, but not as before. The power of evil has been curtailed and could be lessened even more if people would believe the gospel. The devil has been confined (or "tied up" as Jesus indicates in Matthew 12:29), and we may live as people freed from his tyranny. (Now.)

The New Testament teaches that Satan now influences people primarily through fear and trickery, twin devices for a tyrant who is otherwise impotent.

There are many passages in the Bible that encourage us to recognize that Satan is a vanquished foe (1 John 3:8; Hebrews 2:14). His power over us has been broken: his threats are empty, his posture illusory. The simple solution is, "Resist the devil, and he will flee from you" (James 4:7). That old "devil made me do it" excuse just won't work. The devil no longer holds that sort of power over us, and we may live as "more than conquerors," confident in the victory of Jesus Christ (Romans 8:37).

Or so the Bible *sometimes* says. But, then, in other places, the Bible seems to refer to Satan as a very powerful, very active entity who cannot be counted out (1 John 5:19; Ephesians 6:12). "Keep alert," the Scriptures say. "Like a roaring lion your adversary the devil prowls around, looking for someone to devour" (1 Peter 5:8). The devil is said to be responsible for orchestrating the persecution of Christians (Revelation 2:10), for blinding unbelievers to the light of the gospel (2 Corinthians 4:4), for tempting devout Christians to sin (1 Corinthians 7:5), and for setting various snares to trap clergy (1 Timothy 3:7) and laity (2 Timothy 2:26) alike. Even the apostle Paul admits on one occasion that his plans to visit a particular church were thwarted when "Satan blocked our way" (1 Thessalonians 2:18).

These two ideas—that Satan is *both* vanquished *and* powerful—are in tension with each other, and the sense of that tension is captured symbolically through the image of a captured-but-not-yet-terminated tyrant. Notably, the New Testament teaches that Satan now influences people primarily through fear and trickery, twin devices for a tyrant who is otherwise impotent. Thus, believers are warned not to be "outwitted by Satan" or to be "ignorant of his designs" (2 Corinthians 2:11). We are to "put on the whole armor of God" so that we may be able to "stand against the wiles of the devil" (Ephesians 6:11). Ah, yes, the *wiles*. That's what evil is, according to the New Testament: wily. Evil has no real power over us, but it may claim that it does. It's all a trick, the Bible says. "Do not make room for the devil" (Ephesians 4:27).

We are still discussing what theologians mean when they talk about the Already and the Not Yet. We can get in trouble, the Bible suggests, if we fail to recognize the truth in either camp. The power of evil is *already* vanquished, but it is *not yet* terminated. Recognizing both propositions is essential to avoid the wiles of the devil. He would love to have us fear him, since fear is an antidote to love (1 John 4:18) but, failing that, he would also love to convince us that there is no danger at all. He has dug one ditch for the overconfident and another for those who lack confidence altogether, and he would delight to see us tumble into either trench.

## The Two Ages

In one curious passage from St. Paul's first letter to the Corinthians, the apostle refers to the people of his day as those "on whom the ends of the ages have come" (1 Corinthians 10:11). What does *that* mean? What are these multiple ends of multiple ages?

The Bible often speaks of two ages: an old age and a new age. The first is a time of struggle and hardship during which people are sustained by the promises of God for a better tomorrow. The second is a glorious era of salvation during which time God's promises are fulfilled. In the Old Testament, there is talk of a "day of the Lord" when God will act to initiate this wonderful new age (see, for instance, Isaiah 4:2-6; Zephaniah 3:15-20; Zechariah 14:9-20).

Day of the Lord ( Golden age )

OLD AGE                              NEW AGE

The testimony of the New Testament is that something remarkable happened with Jesus Christ, something that no one had been expecting. Jesus came as the agent of God to inaugurate the new age of salvation, but he did *not* bring the old age to a close. As a result, the two ages ended up overlapping each other like this:

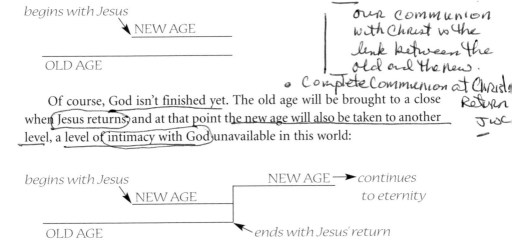

*begins with Jesus*

NEW AGE

OLD AGE

*our communion with Christ is the link between the old and the new.*
*• Complete communion at Christ's Return*

Of course, God isn't finished yet. The old age will be brought to a close when Jesus returns, and at that point the new age will also be taken to another *JWC* level, a level of intimacy with God unavailable in this world:

*begins with Jesus*                    NEW AGE → *continues*
                                                *to eternity*
NEW AGE

OLD AGE                    *ends with Jesus' return*

If this were one of those maps at an amusement park with a big star reading "You Are Here," where would that star be located? For us, it would be somewhere between the first coming of Jesus Christ and the second, during that interval of time when the new age and the old age overlap. This is what Paul means when he says that we are people upon whom "the ends of the ages have come." He means that we live during the overlap.

We must recognize the existence of *both* ages. There are Christians who are so excited about the new life they find in Jesus Christ that they do not reckon with what it means to live in a world that is still subject to death and decay—a world that is "passing away" according to the Bible (1 Corinthians 7:31) but is nevertheless still here. "God will solve our problems," the naïve young Christian will say, "if we only have faith." No. Not yet. There is no promise *yet* that we can enjoy freedom from hardship or trouble. "God showers us with blessings! Why should anyone ever be disappointed or sick or sad?" Why? Because the old age has not yet ended.

> This is what Paul means when he says that we are people upon whom "the ends of the ages have come." He means that we live during the overlap.

But there are also Christians—many of them—who do not seem to realize that the new age of salvation has already begun. "The time is fulfilled," Jesus said (Mark 1:15). God is ready and willing to rule our lives, and, indeed, to shower us with blessings in the here and now. Christians who don't get this are prone to "living beneath their privilege," as the Pentecostals like to say.

The *overlap* is what makes life confusing. It is what makes this world complicated. But that is what we are trying to do: love Jesus in a *complicated* world.

*Today, is the day of Salvation.*

# CHAPTER TEN

# Baptism and Death

C. S. Lewis says that evil always comes into the world in *pairs*.[8] Every problem in life has an opposite—and the opposite is also bad, usually just as bad as the problem we wish to avoid. Gluttony is bad, but so is anorexia. Some people have trouble controlling their tempers, but those who *never* get angry may be simply apathetic or uncaring.

As I hinted in the last chapter, I like to imagine that these pairs of errors are ditches on either side of the narrow path God's pilgrims travel. One can fall into the pit on *either* side of the road. And the devil's favorite trick is to make us fear one ditch so terribly that we will not heed the other. We teeter on the very edge of one chasm, worrying that we might fall into the pit on the other side of the road. Haven't we all known workaholics who take pride in the fact that they are not lazy? Overly strict parents who constantly remind themselves not to be too lax with their children? I sat one time in a congregation of bored parishioners and listened to a monotone preacher read a sermon titled "The Dangers of Enthusiasm." He warned his congregation about snake handlers and holy rollers. I think I agreed with every word he said, but I'm not sure there was anyone present who was struggling to find less animated expressions for their religious zeal.

In the last chapter, we identified two rather broad ditches to be avoided on the pathway of spiritual development. If we want to grow spiritually as people who love Jesus in this complicated world, we must be aware of (1) what God has already done for us, and (2) what God has not yet done but will bring to completion in the future. On the one hand, believing that God is ready and willing to rule our lives in the present helps us to appreciate the joy and wonder of life in the here and now. On the other hand, believing that God will someday rule our lives in a way that we do not yet experience gives us hope to endure trials when this life does not appear to be all that it could be.

This recognition forms the background for understanding two stories from the Bible: the baptism of Jesus and the death of Jesus, as reported in the Gospel of Mark.

## The Gospel Frame

Mark's Gospel is famous for employing a literary device called "framing." Related material is organized around other material in a way that helps to interpret it. For example, in Mark 11, we find the following stories:

**A**–Jesus curses a fig tree because it has no fruit (11:12-14).
**B**–Jesus attacks the temple in Jerusalem, calling it a "den of robbers" (11:15-19).
**A**–Jesus' disciples discover that the fig tree he cursed has withered (11:20-24).

Scholars say that the story of the fig tree forms a "frame" around the story of the temple. The point seems to be that what happens to the fig tree symbolizes what will happen to the temple if it does not "bear fruit."

Some scholars have said that Mark does this a dozen times. Fairly obvious examples can be found in Mark 3:21-35, 5:22-43, 6:7-30, 14:1-11, and 14:53-72. What is most intriguing, however, is the suggestion that Mark places a frame around his entire Gospel, indicating that the whole story of Jesus should be read in light of what happens at his baptism and his death.

***The Baptism of Jesus.*** The story of Jesus' baptism is told in just three sentences. The first sentence (Mark 1:9) sets the scene by telling us that Jesus was baptized in the Jordan River, a famous location from the Old Testament that marks the eastern boundary of the promised land. The book of Joshua recalls God's words to the Israelites as they first crossed this river: "As I was with Moses, so I will be with you; I will not fail you or forsake you"

(Joshua 1:5). At his baptism, then, Jesus experiences a dramatization of God's promise, "I will not fail you or forsake you." The following sentences tell us what happened next:

> Just as he was coming up out of the water, he saw the heavens torn apart and the Spirit descending like a dove on him. And a voice came from heaven, "You are my Son, the Beloved; with you I am well pleased." (Mark 1:10-11)

Basically, we have a list of *three* things that happened:

1. The heavens were torn apart. In the Bible, "the heavens" are usually depicted as the place where God lives. The heavens are often said to open, for example, when God sends rain to the earth (Genesis 7:11). But this is the only time, ever, that they are said to have been *torn*. That, in itself, is very interesting.
2. The Spirit descended upon Jesus. John the Baptist had said that the coming Messiah would baptize people with the Holy Spirit rather than with water (Mark 1:7-8). If Jesus is to do this, he must first be baptized with the Holy Spirit himself.
3. God speaks from heaven and calls Jesus "Son." Thus, from the beginning, Jesus is to be identified as the Son of God (see also Mark 1:1).

Taken together, these three events represent an initial fulfillment of God's baptismal promise never to fail or forsake Jesus. Refusing to be confined to the heavens, God comes to Jesus through the Holy Spirit, affirming that Jesus is God's own beloved child.

**The Death of Jesus**. Near the end of Mark's Gospel, Jesus is crucified. The story leading up to this event is a tale of abandonment (see the chart on page 92). Everyone, it seems, has turned against him: Jews and Gentiles, rulers and peasants, guards and prisoners—even his own disciples.

And then what seems unthinkable, happens. Nailed to a cross, enduring terrible humiliation and suffering, Jesus cries out, "My God, my God, why have you forsaken me?" (Mark 15:34). Has God also abandoned Jesus? What about the baptismal promise, "I will not fail you or forsake you"? What Mark reports next provides an answer to this question:

> Then Jesus gave a loud cry and breathed his last. And the curtain of the temple was torn in two, from top to bottom. Now when the centurion, who

*[handwritten marginal and inline notes:]* Transfiguration stands between as a testimony to God's Promise at Jesus' Baptism, yet directly to to a greater Promise of Resurrection JwC.

• God's glory present
• God's glory yet to come JwC.

stood facing him, saw that in this way he breathed his last, he said, "Truly this man was God's Son!" (Mark 15:37-39)

Again, we have a list of *three* things that happened:

1. Jesus expires, as the breath goes out of him. The English text here is a bit loose. What the Bible literally says is that "the spirit went out of Jesus" (in Greek, the words *spirit* and *breath* are identical). This may bring to mind the reference to the Spirit coming upon Jesus at his baptism. In other words, God gave God's Spirit to Jesus at baptism; now, Jesus gives his spirit to God at death (compare Luke 23:46).

2. The curtain of the temple was torn in two. This reminds us of the heavens being torn apart at Jesus' baptism. In fact, the curtain that hung in the temple was actually a tapestry that had a picture of the heavens embroidered on it. Thus, worshipers in the temple would look at the curtain and see a portrait of the sky. When Mark says that this curtain (with a picture of the heavens) was torn, his readers would surely remember the scene at the beginning of the Gospel when the heavens themselves were torn.

3. The army officer in charge of Jesus' execution proclaims Jesus to be the Son of God. He is the only human character in the Gospel ever to do this, and

---

**THE ABANDONMENT OF JESUS IN THE GOSPEL OF MARK**

- Peter, James, and John fall asleep while Jesus prays in the garden (14:32-40).

- Judas betrays him (14:44-45).

- His disciples forsake him and run away (14:50).

- A young man "leaves all" to get away (14:51; cf. 1:18, 20).

- Jewish leaders mock him as a false prophet (14:65).

- Peter denies Jesus (14:66-72).

- The crowd calls for him to be crucified (15:6-14).

- Roman soldiers mock him as a false king (15:16-20).

- Passers-by join Jewish leaders in mocking him on the cross (15:29-32).

- Crucified criminals taunt him (15:32).

- Jesus cries, "My God, my God, why have you forsaken me?" (15:33-34).

---

his testimony reminds us of the voice at Jesus' baptism that proclaimed him to be God's Son.

Thus, in the very moment that Jesus questions God's faithfulness, that faithfulness seems to be somehow reaffirmed. The events of Jesus' death reprise those of his baptism in a way that suggests the two moments are similar: his baptism is like his death, *and* his death is like his baptism:

At His Baptism:
heavens torn
spirit comes
voice says, "Son"

At His Death:
curtain torn
spirit leaves
voice says, "Son"

## Ending and Beginning

*"Buried with him in Baptism,*
*Raised to new life in Christ."*

Apparently, readers of this Gospel are expected to notice that these two stories are similar and to wonder why that is so. We are invited to compare these two concepts (baptism/death) and ask how they are alike.

*How is baptism like death?* The apostle Paul says, "Do you not know that all of us who have been baptized into Christ Jesus were baptized into his death?" (Romans 6:3). Even today, when a person is baptized in most liturgical churches, the minister will draw a cross on the person's forehead, saying, "[Name], child of God, you have been sealed with the Holy Spirit and marked with the cross of Christ forever." Why the *cross* of Christ—a symbol of death? What Paul and the liturgical churches mean to convey is that baptism is not just the start of something new—it is also the end of something old. The new life in God has begun; the old life apart from God has ended (see 2 Corinthians 5:17).

*How is death like baptism?* At one point in the Gospel of Mark, Jesus actually refers to his death as his baptism and, indeed, he refers to *our* deaths as baptisms as well (Mark 10:38). Death is like baptism because both are experiences through which one passes from one realm of existence to another. What Jesus means to emphasize is that death is not just the end of something old—it is also the start of something new. The old life in this world has ended; the new life in paradise has begun (see Luke 23:43).

*Life with God begins at baptism, but it begins more fully and completely at death.*

93

*[margin notes: Worder & Spirit / Physical birth / Spiritual birth, life anew. JWC]*

There are two endings and two beginnings. Life apart from God may be said to end at baptism, but it ends more definitely and completely at death. Life with God begins at baptism, but it begins more fully and completely at death. Our baptism is a minideath, initiating the beginnings and the endings that will be completed later.

This may sound similar to what we said in the last chapter about the rule of God being both a present and a future reality. The author of Mark's Gospel framed his story about Jesus proclaiming God's rule with stories about baptism and death. Why? Because baptism and death are the moments through which humans often realize the implications of what Jesus said about the world in general:

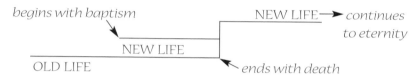

*begins with baptism* — NEW LIFE → *continues to eternity*

NEW LIFE

OLD LIFE — *ends with death*

Just as all Christians live during an overlap of ages (between the first and second comings of Christ), so too the individual Christian lives between two stages of God's salvation, realized in the events of baptism and death. There is, again, an overlap: the old life has not completely ended, but the new life has already begun. *—) but is not yet complete. JWC.*

## Removing Barriers

The most telling part of Mark's story for me concerns the ripping of the heavens and of the temple curtain. These are not just any two items that are torn. Most people in the ancient world thought that God lived either in heaven or in the temple. Thus, the sky and the curtain were barriers that separated people from God. When people looked up at the heavens, they thought, "God is on the other side of that sky," and when they worshiped in the temple, they thought, "God is on the other side of that curtain."

In Mark's Gospel, when first the heavens and then the temple curtain are torn asunder, it is as though God is breaking out of these places where God would be confined. God will no longer live up in the clouds or in a special building. God rips away whatever hides or separates God from mortal beings.

94

*" a temple not made by human hands.*

Mark's Gospel is about a God who invades our space, a God who is no longer confined but loose in the world of people.

*Living Stones built to form a living temple of the living God — whose Spirit dwell in us.*

*JWC*

The ancient world was not so different from our own. If we ask people today, "Where is God?" they will likely respond "in heaven" or "in church." We still refer to God jokingly as "the man upstairs" and we still refer to our local church building as "God's house." When Jesus walked into Galilee claiming, "The time is fulfilled, and the kingdom of God has come near" (Mark 1:15), he meant to dispute such thinking. God does not dwell apart from us. God is *here* and is ready and willing to rule our lives.

Still, we notice that the *moments* when God rips away such barriers are twofold: baptism and death. If we are believers, we have probably experienced the first of these, but if we are still alive, then we have not yet experienced the second. What this means, practically, is that some barriers are gone, while others remain.

I would urge you to make a list of anything and everything that could ever separate you from God. Write down the obstacles and hindrances to your spiritual development. As you try to grow spiritually, as you seek to love God more, what is it that gets in the way?

The good news is that everything on your list will be dealt with in time. The even better news is that many things on your list may have been dealt with already. The not-so-good news is that some things on your list are not going to be dealt with until you die (so you might as well get used to them).

Everything on your list can go in one of two columns: "Removed in Baptism" or "Removed in Death." Of course, knowing which items go where is significant. I can't possibly guess at everything you might put on your list, but let me take a couple of examples.

**Sin.** Many people say, "sin separates me from God." That one should go on the baptism list. We have been washed clean of sin. Our sins have all been forgiven us, and we have been put right with God by sheer, unmerited grace. Your sins do not need to separate you from God or prevent you from loving God or from being loved by God. If you have trouble believing this, read the stories of notorious sinners in Luke 7:36-50 and Luke 18:9-14; in both cases the sinner (*current* sinner, not *ex*-sinner) is a much more spiritual person (an individual who is much closer to God) than the "righteous person" with whom she or he is contrasted.

**Time.** Many people say, "I don't have enough time to pray or read the Bible or do what would help me draw closer to God." Well, that one is here to stay. You may be able to get more organized or to learn some time-management skills (and you probably should), but being baptized does not give you more time. Neither does loving God or believing in Jesus. God is not going to give you twenty-five or twenty-six hours in your day. Not having enough time is a problem that you need to learn to live with, because it is a problem that God is not going to fix for you on this side of death.

Maybe we can make this simpler. Martin Luther believed that there were only three things that are not dealt with in baptism. I don't know if he's right or not, but he seems to be right about some other things, so I think it's worth considering. His short list of matters that are not removed in baptism: the world, the flesh, and the devil.

His first category, "the world," would include the problem of time that we just mentioned and other matters that are intrinsic to living in a finite environment. We are all subject to the laws of nature, and baptism does not change that. Likewise, we may have to reckon with other aspects of living in this world that do not get changed just because they conflict with our spiritual goals. Most of us have to have jobs, whether they are spiritually enriching or not. We also have to learn things like multiplication tables and highway laws, even if they have no obvious spiritual application. Being baptized does not take us out of this world or exempt us from having to be concerned with all sorts of mundane matters.

Luther's second category is "the flesh"; we have weak, mortal bodies that get sick and need sleep and crave things that might not always be good for them. Again, none of that is going to change during this lifetime. No matter how spiritual you become, no matter how close to God you are, you will still have a mortal body subject to fatigue and stress. It will break down, just like the bodies of less spiritual people. You may think, if I had a better body—a spiritual body like the angels—then, I could be *really* close to God. True, but it isn't going to happen, not until Jesus comes for you at the hour of his great return or at the hour of your personal death. So, the weaknesses and the inadequacies of our flesh are something we have to learn to deal with—they are problems that might be managed in this life but that cannot be avoided.

Finally, there is "the devil," and the continuing problem of evil. Baptized people suffer the effects of evil just like everyone else—evil without and evil within. We should not think that if we grow spiritually, we will find ourselves in some protective cocoon where evil cannot touch us. Evil is all around, and catastrophes strike without regard for the spiritual fortitude of those involved. The good and the bad, the wise and the foolish must endure the storms of life; spiritual growth does not help us to avoid such trials, though it might help us to hold up or to keep things together when the storms come (Matthew 7:24-27). And the evil is not only outside of us. The voice of evil speaks within our own thoughts and in the depths of our own hearts. This too is not undone by baptism. The devil will continue to tempt us and will do his best to trick us as long as we live. No matter how spiritual we become, we will never (in this life) reach a point where we no longer have to be on guard against the influence of evil and our own proclivity for it. Indeed, we will never be more in danger than if we think we *have* reached such a point. Even the Beatles knew that "pride goes before a fall"—it's in their song, "I'm a Loser," though they got it from the apostle Paul (1 Corinthians 10:12), who got it from Proverbs (see 16:18).

When we die—or when Jesus comes for us—we will no longer live in this world of space and time, we will no longer have bodies of flesh, and we will no longer have to worry about the effects of evil or the wiles of the devil. For now, we have to put up with stuff like that and try to love God as best we can, given these limitations. But *everything else*, Luther says, has been taken care of in baptism. Guilt? Fear? Pride? Shame? Low self-esteem? A sense of futility or helplessness? Are you greedy? Lustful? Things like that have all been dealt with *already*, and they need not define who you are in relationship with God. Those barriers have been removed. They do not separate us from God any longer.

Believe it! The guilty and the fearful may be very close to God. The proud and the ashamed, the timid and the despairing—all may have rich spiritual lives and be very close to God. The greedy and the lustful—they may love Jesus dearly and be very close to God. Of course, it would be nice *not* to be guilty or fearful or . . . whatever. Of course. And God will keep working on us. But the good news—the *gospel*—is that taking care of such matters (becoming psychologically healthy or morally responsible people) is not a *prerequisite* for developing an intimate and loving relationship with God. If anything, it may be the by-product or *result* of such a relationship. Being flawed persons (dysfunctional, traumatized, or irresponsible) does not prevent us from being spiritual people who love Jesus and who are close to God.

## Walking Wet

So what happens *between* baptism and death? That is the era for what we call "spiritual growth," a time for laying claim to all that God offers us while also recognizing what is not currently on the table. As I have indicated, being in a relationship with God through Jesus Christ does not depend upon our own pitiful attempts at self-improvement. This is the first, and probably the most important, truth of the gospel. When we are baptized, most of the things that would prevent us from being close to God are removed, including the effects of our own sins and inadequacies. We do not have to become better people in order to be close to God and to have rich spiritual lives. Still, spiritual growth is possible, and people who are close to God and who have rich spiritual lives can, in fact, become better people.

I mentioned above that sin need not separate us from God, because our sins have already been forgiven. The baptized are washed clean of sin and are able to experience spiritual intimacy with God as people who have been "justified by faith" and who "have peace with God through our Lord Jesus Christ" (Romans 5:1). But that's not all! In baptism God also gives us the power to overcome sin, to improve our behavior, and to become better people. Theologians debate whether it is hypothetically possible for mere humans to progress to a point of perfection (when they no longer sin *at all*), but we will not bother too much with that question (since it is pretty much hypothetical, anyway). What is certain is that people who confess their sins, repent of their sins, and strive to live better lives can expect to make some progress in that regard. Both the effects of sin and the power of sin are broken at baptism, and we can experience now the practical benefits of a new life that has already begun.

Not everything changes. We still have mortal bodies, we live in a finite world, and evil still exists. It is not realistic to expect *those* things to change. It *is* realistic, however, to expect growth in ways that do not ignore these realities of the human condition. We *can* grow morally, improving our conduct in accord with God's laws. And we can grow psychologically or emotionally: We can achieve victory over guilt or shame or pride or low self-esteem. We can become healthier people. We not only can, but we should, and we not only should but we almost certainly will, for in our baptism God has already removed every impediment to such growth. We act on God's grace, realizing the implications of our baptism and living in accord with the promise and power of God. Luther called this "walking wet."

> We act on God's grace, realizing the implications of our baptism and living in accord with the promise and power of God. Luther called this "walking wet."

*Handwritten margin notes:* "the fruit of righteousness" is watered by the waters of Baptism — JWC. the need to do right to the seed which is planted and nurtured grows into our life in Christ. — JWC

98

We can get in trouble spiritually by denying either the validity of our baptism or the necessity of our death. Sometimes, we fail to recognize what God has done for us and allow our spiritual lives to be derailed by problems for which God has already provided the solution. At other times, we harbor unrealistic expectations, imagining that if we grow spiritually we will rise above problems that are in fact unavoidable for mortal beings who live in this world. As spiritual pilgrims seeking to love Jesus in this complicated world, we require faith to let go of every hindrance God has removed in baptism, strength to deal appropriately with those problems that will be with us till death, and discernment regarding which are which.

---

**SERENITY PRAYER ATTRIBUTED TO REINHOLD NIEBUHR**

This famous prayer has become widely known in abbreviated form (just the first four lines). It is worth citing in its entirety:

> God, grant me the serenity
> to accept the things I cannot change,
> courage to change the things I can,
> and the wisdom to know the difference.
> Living one day at a time,
> enjoying one moment at a time,
> accepting hardship as the pathway to peace;
> taking, as He did, this sinful world as it is,
> not as I would have it;
> trusting that He will make all things right
> if I surrender to His will;
> that I may be reasonably happy in this life,
> and supremely happy with Him forever
> in the next.

---

# CHAPTER ELEVEN

# Jesus Is for Losers

The title for this chapter comes from a T-shirt. I once saw a teenager at a shopping mall wearing a shirt that said "Jesus Is for Losers." At first I thought this was a cynical put-down of Christianity on the part of some adolescent who'd decided he was too cool to be associated with religion. Then I noticed the shirt had a Bible reference in parentheses beneath its bold statement. It was actually a Christian T-shirt, witnessing to the gospel. Of course! Jesus is *for* losers, not against them. Jesus came into this world to dine with outcasts and misfits and to proclaim good news to the disadvantaged, the neglected, the marginalized, and the abused. Tax collectors, harlots, Samaritans, lepers . . . losers, all. Jesus said, *I'm for them,* and "many who are first will be last, and the last will be first" (Matthew 19:30).

Anyone raised in the Christian church has heard the message of God's grace. We are reminded again and again that God's favor toward us is not merited or deserved. God's attitudes and actions toward us are not determined by our ability to measure up. If they were, we would all be in big trouble.

We know this and yet, quite naturally, we want to believe that it is not *all* a matter of grace. Surely, we deserve *something.* Bad as we might be, we can always think of others who are *worse.* In his book *The Great Divorce,* C. S. Lewis tells an imaginative tale about a man who arrives at heaven only to meet a murderer. He is incensed that such a criminal would be admitted. Refusing to share eternity with one who doesn't deserve it, he opts for hell instead.[9]

We believe in grace, but we don't really "get it." Often, stories bring the message home in ways that treatises or sermons never could. The Gospel of Mark is such a story. From beginning to end, it presents Jesus' disciples as recipients of grace. I once played a game with a Sunday school class in which I asked them to name as many stories about Jesus' disciples as they could remember. I wrote these on the board in two columns: a list of "positive stories" where the disciples look good, and "negative stories" where the disciples look bad. At the end, two things stood out: *none* of the positive stories were found in the Gospel of Mark and *all* of the negative stories were found in the Gospel of Mark.

Obviously, what we have in this one Gospel is not all there is to tell. In Matthew's Gospel, Peter is the rock on which the church is built (Matthew 16:17-19). The Gospel of John tells of a "beloved disciple" to whom Jesus entrusts the care of his own mother (John 19:26-27). And Luke continues his story of Jesus with the book of Acts, which relates how Jesus' followers served him as spirit-filled missionaries in the days after Easter. So why does Mark paint so bleak a picture?

Some scholars have reasoned that it had something to do with church politics. Maybe the author of this Gospel belonged to a church that was in conflict with churches started by Jesus' disciples, and he seized the opportunity to besmirch the reputations of people those churches called heroes. Personally, I don't think that seems too likely. Mark calls his book "good news" (1:1). How would attacking the leaders of rival churches qualify as good news? More likely, he is motivated by a spiritual, pastoral concern: he wants to emphasize the grace of God that took hold of these people.

We might name our churches after these disciples and call them saints, but Mark wants us to know that, apart from Jesus, they were just losers like us. They were weak and unworthy human beings who were a disappointment to themselves, to others, and to God. We don't remember them because of what they did, but because of what Jesus did for them and through them.

## From Bad to Worse

A colleague of mine speaks candidly of the "dummy disciple" theme in Mark's Gospel. In this book, the twelve men who would later come to be known as apostles never seem to get anything right. Or, at best, they seem to do only *one* thing right: at the beginning of the story, when Jesus calls them, they leave everything behind and follow him (Mark 1:16-20). Good! But from that point on, it's just one problem after another.

For a long time, the disciples don't even seem to know who Jesus is. They don't realize he is the Messiah or the Son of God, they don't understand his teaching, and they don't seem to appreciate what the mission they have undertaken is all about. For example, after Jesus miraculously stills a storm at sea, his disciples are afraid of him, huddling in the bow of the boat and saying to one another, "Who then is this, that even the wind and the sea obey him?" (Mark 4:35-41). The demons know he is the Son of God (Mark 1:34; 3:11-12), and the multitudes who follow him know that he is able to work fantastic miracles, but his own disciples seem to be a few steps behind everyone else.

At times, the story is humorous. When Jesus is with his disciples in a boat, he tells them, "Beware of the yeast of the Pharisees and the yeast of Herod" (Mark 8:15), using a common metaphor to describe the negative influence that those persons might have on others (compare Matthew 16:12 and Luke 12:1). But his disciples are obtuse literalists. They have not brought enough bread with them for the trip, and they are already thinking that when they get to the other side of the lake, they might have to buy some yeast to make more. So, they decide, Jesus is warning them not to buy any yeast from Herod or the Pharisees.

This is incredibly dense. Neither the Pharisees nor Herod were in the yeast-selling business. And the error is intensified by the fact that in the last few days these disciples have witnessed Jesus feeding five thousand people with just five loaves of bread and four thousand people with just seven loaves. One would think they might have figured out by now that "bread sufficiency" is not a problem. And, if they could just quit thinking about their own stomachs, perhaps they would benefit from the spiritual truth that Jesus seeks to impart.

Obviously disappointed, Jesus rails at them with anger and frustration: "Do you still not perceive or understand? How hard are your hearts? You have eyes—why can't you see? You have ears—why can't you hear? Don't you remember *anything*? I'm not talking about bread! Why don't you understand?" (Mark 8:17-18, 21; paraphrased).

Some readers of this Gospel are frankly shocked to discover that Jesus can be so *annoyed* with his own disciples. But in another instance it is even worse. They fail completely to do something for which he had empowered them, and he rails at them in a fit of exasperation: "You faithless generation, how much longer must I be among you? How much longer must I put up with you?" (Mark 9:18-19).

Christian spirituality consists of being in a relationship with this Jesus. It is, of course, the same Jesus who calls himself "the good shepherd" (John 10:11) and who tells us he is "gentle and humble in heart," offering rest for our souls (Matthew 11:29). But the story Mark tells is also part of the picture, and it is a part that makes our relationship with Jesus *real*. Loving Jesus means loving someone who might sometimes get very annoyed with us, exasperated by our stupidity and appalled at our incompetence. I have to wonder: Am I like these disciples in the Gospel of Mark? And does Jesus sometimes lament how much longer he must put up with me? But he *does* put up with us—that is part of the story too.

Eventually, Jesus' disciples do figure out a few things. It takes half the Gospel and then a lightbulb comes on over Peter's head and he says, "You are the Messiah" (Mark 8:29). Jesus does not appear to be too impressed by this realization (in Mark's version of the story; compare Matthew 16:16-19), and the reason soon becomes apparent. Once the disciples figure out who Jesus is, they draw all the wrong conclusions from what they know. "We're in the money, now!" they seem to think. "We were clever enough to hook up with the Messiah—and that can only mean power and glory and riches for us all!"

> Loving Jesus means loving someone who might sometimes get very annoyed with us, exasperated by our stupidity and appalled at our incompetence.

Jesus talks to them about denying themselves and serving other people, but none of this sinks in. They argue with each other over which of them is the greatest (Mark 9:34), and two members of the group try to get the jump on the rest by asking Jesus to guarantee them the *best* seats in glory (Mark 10:35-37). When Jesus says his destiny is to die on a cross, Peter tries to take over as his campaign manager to secure a more desirable outcome (Mark 8:30-32).

Jesus' response goes beyond exasperation and annoyance: "Get behind me, Satan!" (Mark 8:33). His disciples were dummies; now, they are devils. Coming to faith, believing in Jesus as the Messiah, has not made them better people; if anything, it has made them worse. This is troubling but, again, I think that many of us may know people like this. Some of us may *be* people like this.

It all comes to a head when the group encounters the cross. We might wonder as we read Mark's Gospel: When will the disciples finally get it? When will they come to understand both *who Jesus is* and *what this means for them?* The answer is, when they get to Jerusalem and learn why they have come. Yes, Jesus is the Messiah, but no, he isn't going to bring them all glory and honor. He really is going to be crucified, take upon himself suffering and shame in a final act of service to others.

And, apparently, he expects them to do the same! At the very least, he expects them to follow his example and deny themselves for the sake of other people. A long time ago he had told them that anyone who wanted to be his disciple would have to carry a cross in self-denial (Mark 8:34), but, like so many things he said, that one just went on by them. They didn't get it. Now, they do. And this is how they respond:

- One of them (perhaps the brightest) seizes the opportunity to sell out Jesus and escape with a modest profit of thirty pieces of silver (Mark 14:10-11, 44-45).
- Ten of them run away and desert Jesus, leaving him in the lurch when the soldiers come (Mark 14:29-31).
- One of them (apparently the bravest) hangs in a bit longer than the others until, finally, he swears that he doesn't even know who Jesus is and creeps off into the night, weeping bitterly (Mark 14:66-72). The failure is absolute. The disciples prove to be completely faithless (and useless) to Jesus, and their failure appears to be but the final stage of what had been developing all along. They never did understand what following Jesus really meant, and the more they came to understand it, the less they were able to deliver what was expected of them.

## A Brief Catechism

The story of the disciples in Mark's Gospel becomes most meaningful when we consider the role that is played by Jesus himself. Four points are significant:

1. **Jesus calls the disciples** and gathers them into a community (Mark 1:16-20; 3:34-35). No one ever volunteers to be a disciple in Mark's Gospel. Jesus chooses the people he wants to follow him. Supposedly, he

might have found more capable candidates; he might at least have auditioned the applicants, asked for some references, or done minimal background checks. But, no. His selection of the inept almost seems to have been deliberate. His choice of peasants over scribes, laborers over merchants, tax collectors over priests seems almost calculated to ensure exclusion of the wise, the noble, and the powerful. "I have come to call not the righteous but sinners," he says (Mark 2:17), brazenly defending a policy that would seem likely to eventuate in just the sort of ignominy that does end up occurring.

2. **Jesus enlightens his disciples** with special knowledge and teaching (Mark 4:33-34; 7:17-23). Jesus teaches his disciples the mysteries of the kingdom, explaining his parables to them and instructing them in what we would call "the way of the cross." As we noted, it doesn't seem to make any difference. They don't understand him, and they never seem to get any wiser. A scholar once said, "The amazing thing about Mark's Gospel is that, although Jesus keeps teaching his disciples, they never learn." Well, I would turn that around: the *truly* amazing thing about Mark's Gospel is that, although Jesus' disciples never learn, he keeps teaching them. Simply put: he never gives up on them, no matter how aggravating their dim minds and hard hearts seem to be.

3. **Jesus empowers his disciples** to be holy people of God (Mark 3:14-15; 6:7-13). Jesus gives his disciples the "spiritual authority" they need to triumph over evil. Again, readers will notice that they don't make much use of this authority. Occasionally, they are able to help others (Mark 6:13), but they don't use the power Jesus has given them to overcome the evil in their own lives. They don't become better people themselves. Still, he does not take back what he has given. Rather, he constantly reminds them of the power they have, claiming that they would be able to move mountains if only they would put their faith in God (Mark 11:22-24).

4. **Jesus keeps his disciples** in spite of their complete faithlessness to him (Mark 14:26-27; 16:7). This is surely the most important point of all. Jesus never rejects any of his followers, no matter how inadequate they turn out to be. Even when they desert him, deny him, and leave him to die, even *then* the message that goes out from the tomb on Easter morning is, in effect, "Go, tell Peter and the others that I will be waiting for them in Galilee—I intend to see them there." This is frankly incredible! Why doesn't Jesus rise from the dead angry? Why wasn't ditching him in his hour of need "the last straw"? We might have expected him to fire the

whole lot and find twelve new disciples who would prove *somewhat* worthy of him.

This may be the ultimate illustration of God's grace in action. Jesus calls inadequate people who, despite his assistance, never improve. Indeed, they get worse, until finally, they reject him altogether. Still, he does not reject them.

Martin Luther reflects on what it means to be a disciple of Jesus in his *Small Catechism*. In the explanation of the Third Article of the Apostles' Creed he puts it this way:

> I believe that by my own understanding or strength, I cannot believe in Jesus Christ my Lord or come to him, but instead the Holy Spirit has called me through the gospel, enlightened me with his gifts, made me holy, and kept me in the true faith, just as he calls, gathers, enlightens, and makes holy the whole Christian Church on earth, and keeps it with Jesus Christ in the one, common true faith.

The work that Luther attributes to the Holy Spirit in the life of a believer is almost precisely that which the Gospel of Mark portrays Jesus doing in the lives of his disciples. Jesus calls them through the gospel he preaches, enlightens them with his teaching, gives them power to become holy, and, finally, keeps them when they fail him.

## And Now for the Altar Call

Let's bring the matter home. Imagine that you are like one of those disciples in the story Mark's Gospel tells. You embark on a spiritual trek. You are reading this book—that must mean you have some interest in loving Jesus and in growing closer to God. But all is not well. You know yourself, how mixed your motives are, how compromised your values, how perverse your purest intent. You want to be in a relationship with Jesus—but like the disciples in Mark's Gospel, you might not get what that really means. You read the Bible and listen to sermons, but a lot of it you don't understand, and even what you *do* understand doesn't seem to make any difference. You know that God has given you spiritual power to be the kind of person you should be, but you're *not* that person and, secretly, you're not always sure if you even *want* to be.

For most of us, the crunch will never come with the sort of public humiliation brought upon Jesus' disciples. It comes more quietly, as the poverty of our faith is revealed with secret sins and private shame. Something happens or doesn't happen, and we realize what a sham this all is. We are *not* good people, and we are not really committed to loving God with our whole heart or loving our neighbors as ourselves.

Imagine now that you have taken such a realization to its logical conclusion. You have abandoned the faith, denied Christ, gone into hiding, and sought to put as much distance between you and the "spiritual quest" as possible. It is at that moment that the fearful women who visited the empty tomb come to you with a single message: Jesus is waiting for you to join him in Galilee. It is a bit like an altar call. How will you respond? The invitation is this: you can be closer to God, but it has everything to do with Jesus and nothing to do with you. You *can* be in a relationship with Jesus, but on his terms, not yours. The relationship is based *entirely* on his faithfulness to you and not at all on your faithfulness to him. That's the deal. That was the deal all along, though you just didn't get it.

It's called *grace.* The church talks about grace a lot, but most people don't get it. I think it is possible that no one ever gets it until they have crept off into the night weeping bitterly. Comedian Groucho Marx is famous for having said, "I wouldn't want to belong to any club that would have me as a member." But the kingdom of God is a society for sinners. People like us are the only ones allowed. That's the deal.

Jesus is for losers. The Bible verse quoted on that T-shirt was 1 Timothy 1:15: "Christ Jesus came into the world to save sinners—of whom I am the foremost." So, we *can* be in a relationship with Jesus, but we're not just going to be *buddies*. The relationship he offers us is one of patients to physician, sinners to Savior (Mark 2:7).

Grace does not mean Jesus chooses us *even though* we are such losers. It means he chooses us *because* we are such losers—even the best of us. That's the invitation the women from the tomb are bringing. How will you respond?

## Prayer of St. Teresa of Ávila (1515–1582)

May you be blessed forever, Lord, for not abandoning me when I abandoned you.

May you be blessed forever, Lord, for offering your hand of love in my darkest, most lonely moment.

May you be blessed forever, Lord, for loving me more than I love myself.

May you be blessed forever, Lord, for continuing to pour out your blessings upon me, even though I respond so poorly.

May you be blessed forever, Lord, for drawing out the goodness in all people, including me.

May you be blessed forever, Lord, for repaying our sin with your love.

May you be blessed forever, Lord, for being constant and unchanging, amidst all the changes of the world.

May you be blessed forever, Lord, for your countless blessings on me and on all your creatures.

# CHAPTER TWELVE

# People of Little Faith

I know a woman who became frustrated with her church and with her pastor because she did not feel like she was growing in her faith. "All the pastor talks about is the love of God," she told me. "Every week we hear about how much God loves us. I know that already. And on my way to worship, I drive by another church that advertises its sermons on a sign, sermons with titles like 'Seven Ways To Improve Your Marriage.' I figure if only one of those ways works, that would be a good sermon to hear. But my pastor just talks about how much God loves us, and I already know that. I want to hear sermons that will help me to be a better person."

I suggested she talk with her pastor about this; she did and then got back to me: "He said my problem is I don't understand the grace of God. We don't need to be better people for God to accept us as we are. I told him that I did understand the grace of God, and that I know God accepts me as I am, but I would still like to be a better person. He said, oh, now I know what your problem is. You think that you need to be perfect, but that is unrealistic. No one can ever be perfect. I said, no, I know that I don't have to be perfect. I would just like to be better, even just a *little* bit better. Is that too much to ask?"

We have spent a couple of chapters tracing lessons from the Gospel of Mark. Now, we are going to flip back one book to look at the Gospel of

Matthew. I find it interesting to compare how certain aspects of the gospel story are presented in these different books. The Gospel of Mark presents the disciples of Jesus as total losers, apparently to emphasize the grace of God shown to them through Jesus. The Gospel of Matthew doesn't flinch on that point, but it adds something new: in *this* book, the disciples learn a few things as the story goes along, and they show some progress at becoming better people than they were at the start. Matthew understands grace but is also interested in *growth*. Luke and John, incidentally, are similarly inclined. Luke appends the entire book of Acts to his story of Jesus to demonstrate how ordinary people chosen by Jesus eventually became powerful witnesses who "turned the world upside down" (Acts 17:6). John narrates how the disciples deepen in their relationship with Jesus until he is finally able to say them, "I do not call you servants any longer . . . but I have called you friends" (see John 15:15).

Matthew often tells the same stories that are in Mark but tweaks them a bit to give a slightly different view. Look at these two passages side by side:

| Mark 4:40 | Matthew 8:26 |
|---|---|
| [Jesus] said to them, | [Jesus] said to them, |
| "Why are you afraid? | "Why are you afraid, |
| Have you still no faith?" | you of little faith?" |

It is *almost* the same thing, but not quite. In Mark's account, Jesus wonders whether the disciples have any faith at all. In Matthew's version, he is certain that they have a little, but *only* a little. I hope you're not the sort of person who gets all freaked out over "contradictions in the Bible" and who needs to know "What did Jesus *really* say?" If you are, I can't help you—at least, not with that problem. I'm just reporting what the Bible says and trying to make sense of it. Matthew tells the story of Jesus and his disciples a little bit differently than Mark does, and I suspect that Matthew does this because he wants to teach a different lesson.

## Mountains and Mustard Seeds

Matthew's favorite term for the disciples of Jesus is "people of little faith." The phrase has entered the vernacular of our culture at a popular level, such that people who have little acquaintance with the Bible will sometimes chide each other with the words, "O ye of little faith." Most people probably realize that such language has something to do with the Bible (or maybe Shakespeare), but they don't really know any more than that. It could be a trivia question: Who were the original "people of little faith"? Answer: the disciples of Jesus in the Gospel of Matthew. The phrase is used five times in this Gospel, always on the lips of Jesus, addressing his own disciples:

- **Matthew 6:28-30.** Jesus tells his disciples not to worry about clothing. Look at the lilies of the field! They neither toil nor spin. "If God so clothes the grass . . . will he not much more clothe you—you of little faith?"
- **Matthew 8:23-26.** The disciples are in a boat when a big storm comes up. Jesus is asleep, but they wake him up, calling, "Lord, save us!" He responds, "Why are you afraid, you of little faith?"
- **Matthew 14:28-31.** Peter decides that he wants to walk on water, after seeing Jesus do this. Jesus bids him to try, and he actually succeeds for a moment or two. Then he becomes frightened and begins to sink. Jesus reaches out to grab him, saying, "You of little faith, why did you doubt?"
- **Matthew 16:5-10.** The disciples forget to pack bread when they embark on a trip with Jesus and are worried that they might run out. Jesus says, "You of little faith, why are you talking about having no bread?" Then he reminds them of how he has twice multiplied loaves to feed large crowds of people.
- **Matthew 17:18-20.** A man brings his sick child to the disciples, but they are unable to do anything for the boy. Jesus heals the child, and then the disciples ask him why they had not been able to do that themselves. "Because of your little faith," Jesus says.

From this survey, I'd have to say that people of little faith seem like pretty normal people to me. People of little faith worry about whether they will have enough food to eat or clothes to wear. They become frightened when their lives are in danger. And they sometimes find themselves unable to work miracles or to do the impossible. Such attributes would apply to most people I know.

I notice something else: although Jesus calls attention to the fact that his disciples are people of little faith, he never indicates that there is anything that they can do about this. He doesn't offer to increase their faith, nor does he give them any guidance as to what they might do to increase it themselves. One would think that if "little faith" is what's holding these disciples back, then Jesus would tell them what to do about this problem. But he doesn't. He *points out* their little faith as an explanation for why they are not making progress as quickly as they would like, but he never tells them how they can get *more faith* to remedy that situation.

Instead he says, "If you have faith the size of a mustard seed, you will say to this mountain, 'Move from here to there,' and it will move; and nothing will be impossible for you" (Matthew 17:20). When I hear that, I have to wonder why we don't see mountains flying through the air on a regular basis. The point, I suppose, is that persons with a mustard seed's worth of faith could make mountains move *if that's what God expected of them.* And, obviously, the mountains can be metaphorical.

> Persons with a mustard seed of faith can overcome anything in their life that keeps them from being the persons God expects them to be.

Persons with a mustard seed of faith can overcome anything in their life that keeps them from being the persons God expects them to be. A mustard seed, of course, is very tiny—about the size of a grain of salt. So, Jesus seems to be saying, the *amount* of faith is not what's important; you just need to know what to do with the faith you have. Quit worrying about whether you have enough faith and start asking, "Which mountains does God want me to move?" (on this, see also Luke 17:5-6).

There are mysteries here that I do not claim to understand, but here is what I think: I *think* that God gives to each of us a measure of faith and that this is all the faith that we will ever have (in this life). I like to think that God gave this to me at my baptism, when I was but an infant. At any rate, the Bible teaches that faith is a gift of God (Ephesians 2:8), and so I am not sure that there is anything that we can do to acquire more of it. If God has given you only a little bit of faith, then you will be a person of little faith for the rest of your life. Thank God for the faith that you have—and learn how to use it in ways that will draw you closer to God.

Part of the problem here may be defining what is meant by *faith*, since even the Bible uses the word in different ways. When Paul uses the expression "as your faith increases" (2 Corinthians 10:15), he seems to mean something like "as you become more committed to what you believe and live in accord with those beliefs." Certainly, Christians can and should grow in that sense. Likewise, when religious leaders today speak of "faith development," they are often referring to programs that help people to understand what they believe and to find mature and appropriate ways of acting on those beliefs and applying them in their daily lives. Such programs are helpful, and I would never want to imply that such growth and development *in* faith is unattainable.

Still, the faith that is a gift from God is something other than a system of beliefs or commitments; it is, I think, a basic capacity to trust in God. To some extent, our capacity for such trust may also be affected by our upbringing and by the various traumas we experience (or don't experience) throughout life. But, for me, there seems to have been some core element of trust that has remained constant. I discovered it within me, this modicum of faith. I did nothing to produce it, and, though I might be able to ignore it or even deny its presence within me, I do not think that I could ever be rid of it. It is a gift of God, for which I am unspeakably grateful. Still, I have also found nothing that I can do to increase this basic faith that God gave me, which I have had since I was a child. As a young Christian, I thought that as I "grew in faith" I would find it easier to trust in God. That didn't happen. No matter how much I studied the Bible, no matter how much I prayed, no matter how many sermons I heard, no matter how often I took Holy Communion, trusting God never got any easier—at least not for me. What the Bible study and the prayers and the sermons and the Holy Communion *did* do is this: they helped me to live more faithfully and more productively as a person for whom trusting in God (still) does not come easily.

There are people of great faith. Two of them turn up in the Gospel of Matthew. In chapter 8, Jesus encounters a Gentile army officer for whom faith comes so easily that he sees no need for Jesus to come to his house to heal a sick servant. I know how these things work, he says. Just speak the word and it will be done. Even Jesus is surprised: "In no one in Israel have I found such faith" (Matthew 8:10). Then, in chapter 15, Jesus is accosted by a Canaanite woman who insists that he heal her daughter. He seems inclined to deny her request, but she persists, claiming that she is asking for no more than a few crumbs of mercy. Again, Jesus is surprised: "Woman, great is your faith!" (Matthew 15:28). These are persons for whom faith seems to come easily, persons who view the miracles they expect of God as minor matters. Notably, however, they are not persons whom Jesus calls to follow him. He does not invite them to become disciples nor does he commission them to make disciples of others. (but they did have faith which allowed God to work)

I think I've known people like these two individuals. Most pastors will say *God* that they have met people in their churches whose faith is far greater than their *works*
*is not*
*necessarily*
*God's calling,*
*but as God calls us*
*we must do God's work*

own. It does not follow that such people should *be* pastors or evangelists or teachers or missionaries. They are just people for whom trusting in God seems to come easily. Praise God for such people! They are a blessing and a gift to this world. If you are such a person, I am happy for you, and I am happy because of you (and what you bring to this world). But it's not like that for most of us, and it never will be, in this life.

## Faith Seeking Understanding

The Gospel of Matthew presents Jesus' disciples as people whose faith does not increase. But something else does. As the story goes on, Matthew thinks it is very important to tell us that the disciples of Jesus increase in *understanding.*

- **Matthew 13:10-18.** Jesus laments the fact that so many people "listen, but never understand," but then he tells his disciples that *they* are not like that: "Blessed are your eyes, for they see, and your ears, for they hear."
- **Matthew 13:51-52.** After a long day of teaching his disciples in parables, Jesus asks them, "Have you understood all this?" They answer "Yes," and he likens them to "a scribe . . . trained for the kingdom of heaven."
- **Matthew 16:5-12.** Jesus' disciples completely misconstrue something that Jesus says. He is annoyed with them, but explains what he meant. Then Matthew concludes this story by telling us, "*Then* they understood."
- **Matthew 17:10-13.** The disciples wonder about a prophecy in Scripture regarding the coming of Elijah (which has been fulfilled symbolically by John the Baptist). Jesus answers a bit cryptically, but they get his point: "Then the disciples understood."

Nothing like this ever happened in the Gospel of Mark. Why? I suspect that Mark wanted us to know (like the pastor of the poor woman I was describing at the start of this chapter) that no one can ever be too dumb or too pathetic for Jesus. God's grace has it all covered. Matthew (like the woman herself) knows that, but

> God does not just "accept us as we are" and then leave us that way. God helps us to become better people.

wants to make another point: God does not just "accept us as we are" and then leave us that way. God helps us to become better people.

But how does that happen? A key point, for Matthew at least, seems to be understanding. Perhaps the most famous parable Jesus tells in this Gospel is that of the sower who throws seed on different types of soil, with different results (Matthew 13:3-8, 18-23). Some of the seed never takes root, and even plants that do sprout up get choked by weeds or withered by sun. The seed that does make it, the seed that bears fruit, Jesus says, represents "the one who hears the word *and understands it*" (Matthew 13:23; italics mine).

St. Anselm describes the Christian life as "faith seeking understanding" (*Proslogium*, 1). Theologians often talk about *justification* and *sanctification*. Christians are reconciled to God and belong to God for no other reason than that God chooses them and, in love, sends his only Son into the world that they might be saved by believing in him (John 3:16; Romans 5:1; Ephesians 2:8). This extraordinary act of grace is what theologians call "justification," and anyone who has experienced this grace has faith—indeed, I suspect that they have all the faith that they will ever have, all the faith they will ever need to have (in this life). But the Bible also speaks of what theologians call sanctification, a process by which Christians become increasingly the people who God wants them to be. All who have faith want to grow, and they do so not by getting more faith, but by getting more understanding. The justified seek to be sanctified. Faith seeks understanding.

> All who have faith want to grow, and they do so, not by getting more faith, but by getting more understanding.

All right, this is getting a little heady. My simple proposal is this: Christian growth is not so much a matter of increasing faith as it is a matter of increasing understanding. Let's go with this for a moment and see where it leads.

The first implication of this proposal is that Christian education becomes extremely important. Indeed, the Great Commission given at the end of Matthew's Gospel is to make disciples of all nations by *teaching* people who have been baptized. Teaching—Christian education—seems to be the means through which people become disciples. I do not think it is possible to teach people to have faith—that must happen through a miracle of God's grace. It is, however, possible to teach understanding, especially to people who do have faith. In terms of the church's ministry, this may be the difference between *preaching* and *teaching*: preaching (that is, announcing the wonderful works of God) sometimes ignites faith in people's hearts (Romans 10:14-17); teaching these people about God's extraordinary thoughts and ways sometimes leads to understanding (Ephesians 4:18-21). Both preaching and teaching are important and necessary.

It is quite possible, then, that the pastor in the anecdote with which this chapter began was doing exactly the right thing: proclaiming in his sermons "the old, old story of Jesus and his love." The purpose of such preaching is not to instruct people by telling them things they don't know, but to give public expression to the church's faith in ways that celebrate, affirm, and arouse that faith for all who have gathered. Sermons may, of course, serve different purposes in different settings, but a sermon that is part of a worship service should, above all, inspire people to worship. Still, the woman in our opening anecdote hungered for the sort of *understanding* that leads to Christian growth. This is a legitimate need, but one that would more likely be met through involvement in a good Sunday school class or Bible study program than by simply attending worship services, where the focus is rightly on glorifying God, not meeting her personal needs.

But here is something important: even if understanding is logically linked to teaching and education, it is *not* necessarily linked to the intellectual processes of human reasoning that we might associate with highly educated persons today. Jesus chooses common laborers to be his disciples, not scholars or scribes. He says that the understanding of which he speaks must be given by God (Matthew 13:11), and he explicitly indicates that God does not favor "the wise and the intelligent" in doling out such understanding (Matthew 11:25). Likewise, the apostle Paul maintains that "God chose what is foolish in the world to shame the wise" (1 Corinthians 1:27). So this is not primarily a cognitive process, and those who didn't like school or who didn't do very well at academics or who don't even know (or care) what *cognitive* means have no need to fear. Spiritual growth has little to do with *that* kind of understanding.

Jesus says that the church makes disciples by teaching people "to obey everything that I have commanded" (Matthew 28:20). For Jesus, *understanding* is parallel to *obeying*. People who understand the word of God are people who do what God said to do. In another parable, Jesus says, "Everyone then who hears these words of mine and *acts on them* will be like a wise man who built his house on rock" (Matthew 7:24; italics mine). Compare this comment to what he said in the parable of the sower: in the one story, the person who *acts* on Jesus' words has a secure foundation, and in the other, the person who *understands* the word bears much fruit. It is almost the same point, because "acting on the word" and "understanding the word" are pretty much the same thing.

According to the Bible, spiritual growth is not measured by one's intellectual apprehension of divine truth but by whether one *lives in a way that is pleasing to God.* This will be bad news to some people, who want to be spiritual but who don't really want their lifestyle called into question. I can't do anything about that. It is bedrock, spiritual truth: people experience what it means to be close to God when they become the people God wants them to be. The *good* news is that the Bible tells us how to be such people and promises us divine aid in becoming such people. Anyone can do it, including people who have been given only a little faith and who do not excel at academic or intellectual pursuits.

Again, we are speaking in this book about loving Jesus in a complicated world. The Bible often equates *loving Jesus* with living the way Jesus wants us to live. "If you love me, you will keep my commandments," he tells his disciples (John 14:15). I can appreciate why some people would be put off by this suggestion. Many people who are attracted to Christian spirituality are less enamored of what they take to be outmoded or simply prudish aspects of Christian ethics. You may be thinking, I hope what is supposed to be a discussion of spirituality does not turn into one more pedantic lecture on dos and don'ts. No, no. We'll leave the matter for now and talk about something else. But surely you know that the Bible has a good deal to say about obedience and morality and holiness and repentance. Any discussion of biblical spirituality is bound to wind up raising meddlesome questions of *behavior* and *lifestyle* sooner or later.

# CHAPTER THIRTEEN

# Easter Ambiguity

It is Easter morning. A group of women gather at the tomb and hear the good news that Jesus is risen, just as he said. They run to tell the disciples, overcome with what the Gospel of Matthew calls *fear and great joy* (Matthew 28:8). The disciples respond to this invitation, coming to Jesus in Galilee where they *worship and doubt* (Matthew 28:17). Do you know what Matthew is talking about? Have you ever felt fear and great joy, both at the same time? Have you ever worshiped and doubted, both at the same time?

Matthew's Gospel offers a vision of what I call "ambiguous spirituality for ambiguous times." Mature piety, it seems, lies in the reconciliation of elements that are often thought to be irreconcilable—and by *reconciliation* I do not mean "figuring things out so that they are no longer contradictory." Rather, mature piety often involves learning to appreciate paradox so that we are energized rather than depleted by tensions that seem to pull us in opposite directions. Herein lies another point for spiritual growth, for adoption of what I call "the second naïveté" (see page 12).

I once thought, or probably just assumed, that as I grew closer to God I would come to a fuller understanding of spiritual truth as something that was clear and consistent. There were many things about faith that seemed confusing, but I figured the confusion would lessen as I became more spiritually attuned. I have not discovered that to be the case. In fact, I now understand that spiritual truth is *not* clear and consistent; by its very nature, it is often ambiguous and contradictory.

# Fear and Great Joy

What does it mean to experience fear *and* great joy—and to experience both simultaneously?

In Matthew's Gospel, *joy* is usually a positive quality. The magi are "overwhelmed with joy" when they worship Jesus and open their treasures to provide him with gifts (Matthew 2:10). Jesus tells a parable about a man who finds treasure in a field and "in his joy he goes and sells all that he has and buys that field" (Matthew 13:44). In yet another parable, Jesus says that at the final judgment, the Lord will return and say to faithful servants, "Enter into the joy of your master" (Matthew 25:21). So joy is a characteristic of God's kingdom. It is a good thing not only because it is pleasant to experience, but also because it serves as a positive motivating force. People do godly things when they are filled with joy.

What is true for Matthew's Gospel is consistent with what we find in the Bible as a whole. "The joy of the Lord is your strength," Nehemiah told the people of Israel (Nehemiah 8:10). Psalmists long for the joy of God's salvation (Psalm 51:12), declare that "fullness of joy" is found in God's presence (Psalm 16:11), and promise that "weeping may linger for the night, but joy comes with the morning" (Psalm 30:5). Joy is a fruit of the spirit (Galatians 5:22) and a mark of those who love the Lord Jesus (1 Peter 1:8). Jesus himself was able to bear the horror of the cross "for the sake of the joy that was set before him" (Hebrews 12:2).

But this is not the whole story. Sometimes the Bible associates *joy* with faith that is only superficial. The clearest example is found in that parable of the sower to which we made reference in the last chapter. The seed that bears fruit represents the one who "hears the word and understands" (Matthew 13:23), that is, who acts on it and does what is expected. But the seed that falls on rocky soil is like one who hears the word and "immediately receives it *with joy;* yet . . . has no root, but endures only for a while, and when trouble or persecution arises . . . falls away" (Matthew 13:20-21). So joy can be shallow—a veneer that looks pretty and feels nice but that lacks real substance and can be easily removed. J. R. R. Tolkien refers somewhere to what he calls "a joy as poignant as grief." I've always liked that expression. People who experience grief say that it goes to the core of their being. I want joy to be like that. So, in Matthew, Easter worship is an experience of joy mixed with fear.

Fear is not always a positive quality in Matthew, but it *is* often connected with worship: the disciples of Jesus are terrified when they see Jesus walk on water, but then a moment later, they worship him as the divine Son of God (Matthew 14:33). Peter, James, and John are filled with fear when they hear a voice from heaven at the transfiguration, but they respond by falling on their faces in worship (Matthew 17:6). And the centurion and the soldiers at the cross are filled with fear when they behold the stupendous events accompanying Jesus' death, but this brings them to confess, "Truly this man was God's Son!" (Matthew 27:54).

Again, this is true for the Bible as a whole. We are commanded to fear God (1 Peter 2:17) and are told that all will be well with those who fear God (Ecclesiastes 8:12). The Bible says repeatedly that "the fear of the Lord is the beginning of wisdom"—an interesting thought in light of the last chapter's emphasis on *understanding*. Those who fear God, the Bible says, "have a good understanding" (Psalm 111:10).

So, what does it mean to "fear God"? In a simple, profound sense, it means never to forget with whom we are dealing. In one startling passage, Jesus says, "Do not fear those who kill the body but cannot kill the soul; rather fear him who can destroy both soul and body in hell" (Matthew 10:28). I don't think this means that we should worry that God might renege on grace and damn us all to hell, but it might imply a healthy recognition that God *could* do that—or anything else that God might decide. In his children's stories about the land of Narnia, C. S. Lewis chose a lion to serve as an image of Christ. Aslan the lion is good, and the children learn to trust him, but they never forget that he is a *lion*. He's not tame. He's not their pet. What if he should suddenly decide to eat them? The children come to trust Aslan, but they never cease to fear him. And in another book—a more reflective piece for adults—Lewis simply asks, "What do people mean when they say, 'I am not afraid of God because I know He is good'? Have they never been to a dentist?"[10]

> We ought not get too cozy with God. People who get cozy with God experience joy but no fear; they have no root, and when trouble comes, they are likely to fall away.

We ought not get too cozy with God. People who get cozy with God experience joy but no fear; they have no root, and when trouble comes, they are likely to fall away. So, at Easter, we have the combination of *fear* and *great joy*. They go together. Joy is what turns fear into worship; fear is what prevents joy from being shallow.

## Worship and Doubt

The Easter story continues with these words: "The eleven disciples went to Galilee, to the mountain to which Jesus had directed them. When they saw him, they worshiped him; but some doubted" (Matthew 28:16-17). And then Jesus responds with words that are commonly called the Great Commission, sending these worshiping, doubting disciples out to make disciples of all nations and promising to be with them always to the end of the age (Matthew 28:18-20).

Let's focus on these words: *they worshiped him; but some doubted*. As a minor point, I want to note that the word *some* is not actually found in the Greek Bible. Why is it in the English version? Well, Matthew uses a particular construction here that allows translators to think that the word *some* could be implied. He also uses that construction in seventeen other instances, though no one ever seems to think the word is implied in those cases. It *could* be implied here, but why would it be? I asked a Bible translator that question one time and got the following response: "The verse wouldn't make sense otherwise. No one can worship and doubt at the same time." I invited this fellow to visit a Lutheran church. We do it all the time.

I am always intrigued when people assume that the Bible cannot possibly mean what it says and so try to make it say something different. Every now and then they might be right, but usually I think the Bible means exactly what it says, and figuring out *why* it says what it does is a big part of understanding the thoughts and ways of a God who says, "My thoughts are not your thoughts, nor are your ways my ways" (Isaiah 55:8). I think, in Matthew 28:16-20, the Bible says that Jesus gives his Great Commission to disciples who both worship him and doubt him at the same time. If we think that no one can do this, we have a lesson to learn.

But what if I'm wrong? I don't want to base everything that follows on some idiosyncratic reading of a particular verse of Scripture—and there is no good reason why you should trust my interpretive exegetical skills over those of the translators responsible for whatever English Bible you are accustomed to using. So, let's just assume I'm wrong, and the verse really should read "they worshiped him; but *some* doubted." The point still stands. Jesus did not separate out the disciples: "worshipers, stand here; doubters over there." He did not commission the worshipers and rebuke the doubters. No, Jesus gave the Great Commission (with his promise of abiding presence) to worshipers and doubters alike; he gave the Commission to a *community* of disciples in which worship and doubt were allowed to coincide.

I do think it is interesting to note that in the Gospel of Matthew, Jesus' disciples only worship him twice. Also, in Matthew (and, for that matter, the entire Bible), Jesus' disciples are only said to doubt him twice. Guess what? They are the same two times! One is here in Matthew 28:17; the other is in Matthew 14, when Peter tries to walk on water. Do you remember that story? At first, he looks like he's going to make it, but then he sees the wind and the waves and he is frightened. He takes his eyes off of Jesus, and he begins to sink. "Lord, save me!" he cries out. And the Lord does. Jesus takes him by the hand, pulls him up, and says, "You of little faith, why did you *doubt*?" (italics mine). And, then, they get in the boat and the disciples worship Jesus, saying, "You are the Son of God."

Matthew doesn't seem to think it odd for worship to be accompanied by doubt. He at least allows for those two things to go together. In this book, the twelve disciples

- never worship Jesus without doubting him; and
- never doubt Jesus without worshiping him.

Why is this? We should at least notice that, while doubt keeps people from walking on water, it does not keep them from worshiping or from being commissioned by Jesus for a mission to the world. But I think there could be more to it than that.

Worship is of course a good thing, and we need say only a little more about it at this point. I have listed the several verses that speak of worship in Matthew's Gospel (page 124). Again, English Bibles don't always get this right—they sometimes use weak language to say that someone "knelt before" Jesus or "paid homage to him" in places where Matthew almost certainly meant the Greek word (*proskyneō*) to be read as "worship."

Basically, worship seems to be of three sorts. First, people worship to show their reverence before the Lord when they have a request to make. For example, a leper comes to Jesus, worships him, and then says, "If you choose, you can make me clean" (Matthew 8:2). What is interesting about these instances is that the worship always *precedes* the request: Matthew wants to present worship as the proper context for prayer and to show that those who approach Jesus deem him worthy of worship regardless of whether their particular needs are met.

A second type of worship is found when people praise and glorify God after something wonderful has happened. What is interesting about these accounts is that, in every instance, the ones who give thanks do so for what God has done for *others*, not themselves. I wouldn't make too much of this— it's not a consistent pattern elsewhere in the Bible (see Luke 17:11-16)—but Matthew may be prompting us to remember to be thankful not only for what God does for us but also for what God does for others.

A third type of worship is what interests me most. On several occasions, people worship simply because they are aware of God's majesty and presence. They are awestruck and, I think, overcome with a degree of devotion. This is pure worship, corporate love, expressed (always) by a *group* of people who are caught up in the splendor of a divine moment and who become connected to the very heart of God. I would note also that such worship seems to have a strong element of "mystery" to it; perhaps this mystery is what allows for doubt, allows worshipers who know that they do not know everything and who do not need to know everything to recognize that they are in the presence of God.

I think that worship is the essence of spirituality. But worship, like joy, can sometimes be superficial. In Matthew 15, Jesus tells the Pharisees that they worship God with their lips while their hearts are far from God. The Pharisees, of course, are often the fall guys in this Gospel and they seem to *stay* in trouble the whole time. Still, say what you will about the Pharisees—the one thing they never do is *doubt*. They are always certain about everything. They are the "God said it, I believe it, that settles it" people of the Bible. It never occurs to them that they might have overlooked something or misunderstood something. As a result, they are often wrong, but they are never in doubt.

By contrast, disciples of Jesus worship and doubt at the same time—and Jesus doesn't call *their* worship superficial. It might be going too far to say that doubt is a *good* thing, but I do note that Jesus never rebukes anyone for it. I am tempted to believe that, just as fear seasons joy, so doubt seasons worship. Joy without fear becomes shallow, and worship without doubt can be self-assured and superficial. *Fear* and *doubt* are not good things in themselves, but they do keep us grounded in reality.

Mark 16:8 - "... they were afraid."

---

**WORSHIP IN THE GOSPEL OF MATTHEW**

Reverence/Submission:
- A leper worships Jesus, desiring to be cleansed (8:2).
- A ruler worships Jesus, wanting him to restore his daughter to life (9:18).
- A Canaanite woman worships Jesus and asks him to heal her daughter (15:25).
- The mother of James and John worships Jesus and requests special positions for her sons (20:20).

Praise/Thanksgiving:
- Crowds glorify God after Jesus heals a paralytic (9:8).
- Jesus gives thanks to the Father for revealing to infants what is hidden from the wise and the intelligent (11:25).
- A crowd glorifies the God of Israel after Jesus heals many people (15:31).

Devotion/Awe:
- The magi worship Jesus as one born King of the Jews (2:11; cf. 2:1).
- Disciples worship Jesus as the Son of God (14:33).
- Children praise Jesus as the Son of David in the temple (21:15).
- Two women worship the risen Jesus (28:9).
- The disciples worship the risen Jesus (28:17).

---

# Seeking the Kingdom

Some people have a hard time ascribing any positive role to doubt. They think it is the opposite of faith, and something that must always be avoided or overcome. Well, there is something to defining terms. Some English Bibles use the word *doubt* in James 1:6-8 to describe a quality of instability or double-mindedness that hinders progress in faith and prayer. But in the original Greek, the word James uses (*diakrinomai*) is a different word than that used for the doubt that Jesus' disciples exhibit in Matthew's Gospel (*distazō*). I would agree that the quality James is describing is a character flaw, a personality trait that *should* be avoided or overcome. Likewise, when the subject of *doubt* comes up, many people think of the story of Thomas, the disciple who refuses to believe in the resurrection until he sees the risen Jesus for himself. But, again, the Greek New Testament never says that Thomas *doubts* (though some English translations might say this): the Greek expression used means "refusing to believe" (*apistos*). Personally, I think there is a difference between "doubting" and "refusing to believe." As I understand the matter, true *doubt* is what someone experiences when they are trying to believe, but just can't get there. Thomas does the opposite: he tries *not* to believe—and Jesus rebukes him for his stubborn, obstinate ways (see John 20:27).

The doubt that typifies the disciples of Jesus in Matthew's Gospel, the doubt that blends with worship, is not just indecision or obstinacy. Rather, this doubt seems to be a defining character trait for people of little faith. This doubt is the quality of those who are seeking the kingdom (Matthew 6:33), as opposed to those who are sure they have found it. Such doubt is almost encouraged by Jesus when he says, "Ask, and it will be given you; search, and you will find; knock, and the door will be opened" (Matthew 7:7). The invitation to doubt is an invitation to

> The church for Matthew is a community of worshiping doubters, a gathering of people of little faith pooling their mustard seeds together, ready to use those seeds, which seem so insignificant, to move mountains.

*try* to believe even if you are not completely able to do so. On this, see also the prayer of the desperate man in Mark 9:24: "I believe; help my unbelief!"

We have said that Matthew portrays disciples as "people of little faith." This is not tragic, because a "mustard seed" of faith is sufficient (Matthew 17:20). But how much is that? We know it is just a little speck, but how do I know if I have even that much? How much is a mustard seed? Well, here is the answer: enough to worship. Not enough to walk on water or to worship without doubt. Just enough to worship. If you are able to worship God—with all sorts of unanswered questions and unaddressed doubts intact—then you're there.

The church for Matthew is a community of worshiping doubters, a gathering of people of little faith pooling their mustard seeds together, ready to use those seeds, which seem so insignificant, to move mountains. And it is to such as these that Jesus says, "Go therefore and make disciples of all nations, baptizing them in the name of the Father and of the Son and of the Holy Spirit, and teaching them to obey everything that I have commanded you" (Matthew 28:19-20). It is to these that he says, "I am with you always, to the end of the age" (Matthew 28:20).

I suspect there is a good reason why the Bible offers worshiping doubters as the ideal paradigm for those who receive the Great Commission. Doubters (worshiping ones, that is) always make the best evangelists. Have you ever heard the testimony of someone who has no doubt . . . who is certain that he or she has found the kingdom:

> Before I knew Jesus, my life was a mess. I was on drugs. Or maybe I drank too much. I was unfaithful to my spouse. I couldn't keep my kids in line. I was mean to the dog. I lost my job. I was unhappy and bitter. I was a real mess. But then I found Jesus and he turned me into the wonderful person that I am today. And I'm here to tell you the good news: if you accept Christ into your life, you can be just as together as I am. Your life can be as good as mine.

These people do not make good evangelists. The apostle Paul said that when *we are weak*, then *God is strong* (1 Corinthians 1:26—2:5). This means that we can only testify to Jesus as people who *don't* have it all together, as people whose lives are *still* a bit of a mess, indeed, as people whose *spiritual* lives are still a bit of a mess, whose joy is mixed with fear and whose worship is mingled with doubt.

Let's return briefly to a point I made in the third chapter of this book. A critical problem in spiritual growth is that we naturally seek a relationship with a God who is a figment of our imagination, rather than coming to know the true God who may or may not fit our expectations. As long as we assume that God really is the way we would like for God to be, we will not have to deal with pesky problems like *fear* or *doubt*. But almost anyone who has gone further, who has sought to discover what the true God made known to us in Jesus Christ is really like, will testify that joy is sometimes seasoned with fear, and faith with doubt. Such an experience is not necessarily as pleasant as a cozy relationship with a God who meets our expectations, nor can faith in such a God be marked by an understanding of spiritual truth that is always clear and consistent. But this is a God we can love. Love is not always cozy, not always pleasant, and not always clear or consistent. Love can be challenging, contradictory, and difficult. It is by nature ambiguous. Loving God—or loving Jesus—in a complicated world means embracing that ambiguity and experiencing the contradictory realities of fearful joy and doubting worship.

# CHAPTER FOURTEEN

# Sunday Morning

A Pentecostal pastor once told me a story about worship. At the time, I didn't get why it was about worship, but now I do. He said: I grew up in a small town, and when I was about ten years old my mother sent me to the florist to pick up some flowers for the dinner table. I was terribly embarrassed to be a boy carrying flowers through the streets of my town; I worried that my friends would see me and tease me or call me a sissy. Six years later, I was in love with a young woman, and I saved some money and I went to that same florist and bought her a bouquet. As I carried it through the streets to her home I never once thought about what anyone would think or say if they saw me. I thought only of her, and of how happy she would be to get flowers and of how delighted I was to be the one to bring them to her.

A famous theology book by Evelyn Underhill argues that worship in its purest form is no more and no less than *adoration*.[11] I had to read the book in college, when it was over my head, and I checked it out again recently only to discover that it's *still* over my head. That Underhill—she sure did know some big words. She has a lot to say about ontological transcendence, whatever that is, but I will always remember this one, basic point: to worship God is to adore God. So much *else* goes on in what we call a "worship service" that it is easy to forget this, or to fail to realize it in the first place. Worship is the corporate expression of the church's love for God. When we worship God, we *love* God, as a community, together. We can love God as individuals, but *worship* is something more. Worship is corporate love.

# The Lord's Day

A few years back I wrote a book about Christian rock music. I got to interview a lot of interesting people: a few celebrities and artists, but they weren't so interesting; the *fans*—they were a trip! I remember being at an outdoor rock festival, and there was a young man with pink hair and multiple body piercings waving his hands above his head and singing of his love for Jesus. I talked to him afterward. "I love Jesus so much," he said to me. "Jesus is my *life*, man, my whole life!" I asked him what church he was from, and he looked at me, puzzled. "No, man, I don't really do church, you know. It's Jesus, that's what it's about. Just Jesus."

Well, I could have argued theology with the poor soul, given him the content of chapters 4 to 5 of this book, explained how the Gospel of Matthew connects the abiding presence of Jesus in our contemporary world with the community of believers known as the church (page 33) . . . but I let him go. I do get what he means, I think. A professor by the name of Diane Jacobson has helped me to get it even more by listing, in David Letterman fashion, the Top Ten reasons why Christianity—as opposed to just Jesus—is unattractive to people in their teens and twenties. The Number One reason, she says, is . . . "It's *boring*!" But why is that an issue now? I'm not sure that church has suddenly become significantly *more* boring than it used to be. I suspect, rather, that in an entertainment-saturated environment, for something to be *boring* is regarded as a much more serious offense than was once the case.

I do admit that a lot of what happens in most churches on most Sunday mornings is pretty boring. It varies from community to community, and a lot of things can be rendered less boring for worshipers who are better instructed in liturgy and faith. Still, if one is concerned primarily with making the best use of one's time, with investing every hour of life in something that will be

> Worship is the corporate expression of the church's love for God. When we worship God, we *love* God, as a community, together.

128

*no one ever died from boredom, but some have died as a witness to Jesus Christ. JWC*

TOP TEN REASONS CHRISTIANITY IS NOT ATTRACTIVE
TO TEENS AND TWENTY-SOMETHINGS

10. It is out of fashion—it's not what people on television and in magazines do.

9. It is irrelevant to our daily lives.

8. It is cumbersome and hard to understand.

7. It is not an *immediate* concern. Attention to this can be postponed until there is more time.

6. It doesn't seem to hold up against science and history.

5. It is too public—religion should be a private matter.

4. It is too absolute—truth is relative and a matter of personal opinion.

3. It is too authoritarian—I don't want anybody or anything telling me what to think.

2. It is all about morality that is outmoded and hypocritical. Even people who claim to believe it don't practice it.

AND, the Number One reason that Christianity is not attractive to Teens and Twenties . . .

1. It is boring.

(Derived from a lecture by Diane Jacobson.)

rewarding or at least interesting, attendance at Sunday morning church services may sometimes be hard to justify.

I remember talking to *another* Christian rock fan down in Austin, Texas. He was a Jesus freak, just like I used to be and still want to be, and I envied him. He was just living in the joy of the Lord, reading his Bible every day and praying to Jesus and speaking in tongues and playing Christian rock on his stereo. When I asked him about church, he didn't write it off, but he did say that he hadn't been able to find a congregation where he felt like he fit in. "The church where I'm a member," he said, "it's like something out of an old black-and-white TV show. You know, *Ozzie and Harriett* or *Leave It To Beaver*. Everybody dresses up in suits, and they play this music that doesn't sound like anything on the radio and the preacher talks about things that have *nothing* to do with my life, and, I don't know, it's just . . . *boring!*" So, he said, he didn't go. I asked him about finding a different church, but he didn't know about denominations and didn't really want to get into all the different doctrines and stuff, so he just didn't go anywhere. "Maybe when I'm older, I'll get more out of it," he said. "Or maybe the church will, you know, lighten up or something."

Well, this time, I did give advice. I don't know if it was *good* advice or not, but I thought about it overnight and then I got back to him:

"Do you love Jesus?" I asked.

"Yes, I do. I love him with all my heart."

"Would you die for him?"

"Yes, I would."

"You would die for him, but you won't be bored for him?"

And so I said, this is what I think the Lord wants you to do: I think that Jesus wants you to get out of bed every Sunday morning and go to the *Ozzie and Harriet* church and just sit there for one hour, being bored. Do it for him. Call it "bearing your cross" if you like. Just do it.

Good advice? Or not? Well, I'll tell you a bit more of my own story and the reasons that I think this way.

When I was a young pastor just arriving at one of the churches I had the privilege to serve, I was told that the congregation wanted me to visit the "inactive members" (persons who had quit coming to church). I was supposed to call on them and see if I could win any of them back. I now know that experts in pastoral ministry say the evangelism of inactives is exceedingly difficult, but I didn't know that then and I committed myself to visit one inactive family a week for a year. I didn't win many people back (on that point the experts were right), but I did hear some stories. For an entire year, I sat in homes and listened to people tell me why they had quit coming to church. Of course, I looked for patterns, but the reasons were diverse: some people thought the church was too liberal (or too conservative); some didn't like the liturgy (for example, the "new hymnal"); some didn't like the youth program, or the way we did Communion. People said, "I wasn't getting fed" or "I just didn't feel inspired" or "The people weren't very friendly" or "I thought it was boring." It took me a while to find the common denominator: everyone was saying in some way, shape, or form, "I quit coming to church because I wasn't getting out of it what I thought I should get out of it."

Now this struck me as odd. When I was little, my mother used to pile us in the car every Sunday morning and drive us to church, and she would say, "We are going to worship God." I always thought that *that* was why people went to church: to worship God. But these inactive members, apparently, did not have mothers like mine, and they had all somehow gotten the idea that the *reason* one goes to church is to get something out of it. Frankly, as a child, I'm not sure if I ever expected to get anything out of it or not. At any rate, that wasn't the point. "Six days a week, God is good to us," my mother would say, "and on Sundays we give thanks."

Where do we get the idea that what happens in church is about *us*? It is the Lord's day. We go to worship the Lord.

Back in 1997, my oldest son David was awarded the Eagle Scout badge in Boy Scouts. I'm not sure if you know what a big deal this is—I didn't, and I am an Eagle Scout myself. I think that when I got the badge, they just handed it to me at one of our weekly scout meetings. They do more than that now. The scout troop rented a hall for a big ceremony on a Sunday afternoon. Printed invitations were mailed out and leaders from the community came to participate. David's teachers and scout leaders and even someone from the mayor's office took turns standing up and saying great things about David. It was his day. Somehow, I doubt that anyone went home from that occasion saying, "I didn't get much out of that. Nobody paid any attention to my needs. They didn't run the ceremony the way that I would have liked." Do you know why nobody said that? Because it wasn't their day. It was David's day. People were there for one reason only: to honor David.

Sunday is the Lord's day. We gather to honor our Lord. Do we measure the quality of a worship service by how much it blesses us? Think again! Six days a week God blesses us, my mother would say. Is it too much to ask that one day—one *hour*—we set aside to say "Thank you?" But, no. We want to get blessed during *that* hour too! And if we don't, well then, we just won't come anymore.

So, it dawned on me that *this* is the common denominator for all inactive members. They never knew the reason for going to church in the first place. They thought it was for them, not for God. They somehow never understood that what we do in church is *worship*.

And then it struck me that people who *do* attend might not get this either. I began asking the *active* members of my congregation why they came, and I would hear references to exciting programs, inspiring sermons (didn't hear that one too often), and the joy of Christian fellowship. Not bad answers, but I began putting those folks on a "potential inactive list" because, of course, all those things can change. What will not change is this: God is worthy of worship. That will not change. And no one so far has ever told me, "Well, pastor, I quit coming to church because I decided that God just isn't really worthy of being worshiped any more." I have never heard anybody say that.

131

# Why This Waste?

Pastors and other church leaders work hard to create Sunday morning programs that will be enriching and meaningful to everyone who attends. Much of the traditional liturgy is in fact directed to the congregation, not to God: provocative sermons, edifying music, words of Scripture, benedictions of peace. My own tradition often speaks of Sunday morning as the occasion for people to receive the divine gift of forgiveness of sins that is mediated through word and sacrament. All of this is very important, but all of it is secondary. Receiving such blessings should not be the *reason* why we come; indeed, we are more likely to receive such blessings when they are *not* the reason why we come.

That was the idea behind the advice I gave the Austin Jesus freak: don't go to that boring church because of what you hope to get out of your experience there; go because you love Jesus and want to worship God. Then, see what happens. Waste an hour on Jesus—and see what happens.

Do you remember the story in the Bible where the woman pours a whole jar of cologne all over Jesus' feet (Mark 14:3-9)? "Why this *waste*?" the disciples complain. The ointment could have been put to some more practical use. A valid point—but the woman hadn't thought of that. Likewise, someone might have told the sixteen-year-old who'd just bought flowers for his girlfriend that he could have spent his money on something more practical—she probably needed school supplies more than flowers. The thing is, people who are in love are seldom pragmatic. They waste their time and their money and everything else on the object of their affection. So if you think church is boring, then you have an excellent opportunity for experiencing worship at its best: as a complete waste of your time, of your intellect, of everything you value . . . all for the one you love. Just open that jar, filled with all of your ideas about what is rewarding and worthwhile, filled with *your* thoughts and *your* ways . . . and upend it on the feet of Jesus. When people around you are saying "Why this waste?" then you'll know you've got it right.

If I were the pastor of a congregation right now, I would tell my people, "This hour is for adoring God, for praising Jesus Christ, for giving thanks to our Lord who is so good to us. That is why we are here. That is what we have come to do. If *you* get blessed, it's a bonus, a by-product. It's nice when that happens. We hope it happens a lot—but it's not why we're here. This is the Lord's day, and we have come to worship the Lord."

But I'm not a pastor of a church right now—I'm just a *member* like most of you. And I have learned what it feels like to lie in bed on Sunday morning, especially after being out late on Saturday night. Why should I get up and go to church? When I've only had five hours of sleep and I've already hit the snooze button a couple of times, why should I get up, put on a suit (they still wear those in my denomination), and drive across town to go to church?

It's a good question, and I've got to tell you, most of the things my pastor and my church's worship leaders work so hard to accomplish don't ultimately have a lot to do with the answer I give. I'm not putting them down, either. We have a fine handbell choir at our church, but I'm just not going to get out of bed, put on a suit, and drive across town to hear them. Our pastor is a good preacher, but what with television and the Internet, inspiring sermons can be accessed at more convenient times than Sunday morning. No, if the question I asked myself on those hazy Sundays was "Am I going to get something out of church this morning to make it worth my while to attend?" I suspect I might end up hitting that snooze button a few more times than I do. But that's not the question. I ask, "Does God deserve to be worshiped?" That's a different question, and the answer seems unaffected by such matters as when I got to bed last night, or whether the pastor is on vacation and we are having a guest preacher, or whether it's the last week of May and we don't turn the air-conditioning on until June, or any number of other factors.

In chapter 2 of this book I talked about what Christians call *piety* and about how that term seems to get a bad rap in our current day. It gets associated with all kinds of things like hypocrisy and superficiality and judgmental intolerance. Be that as it may, the word *piety* literally means *duty*. Pietists believe that worshiping God is a duty, something that we owe God because God deserves it. This concept has fallen on hard times because the ethos of our era emphasizes *sincerity*: you shouldn't do something unless you really feel like doing it; otherwise you are insincere. Well, obviously, no one wants to go to church week after week just pretending to give expression to a faith that is not really there. Still, I cannot imagine anyone growing spiritually or coming closer to God without some appreciation for the value of *duty*. Sometimes we do something because it is the right thing to do, whether we feel like doing it or not.

And there's something else: spiritual growth, we have said, involves being in a relationship with a God who is capable of surprising us. If we only do "what we feel like doing," we will rarely be surprised by the outcome. That's *another* reason I gave the Austin Jesus freak the advice I did: I've come to trust in a God of surprises and I think it likely—*very* likely—that if he were to start attending that boring *Ozzie and Harriet* church out of a sense of duty or piety or whatever you want to call it, he would be surprised by a God whose ways are not his ways. I can't say how, because God's ways aren't *my* ways, either, but I believe he would be. Plus, his congregation sounded like a church that could use a Jesus freak or two in their midst, and I suspect that if he had begun attending, God might have used him to bring some surprises to others. C. S. Lewis said, "Dogs and cats should always be brought up together—it broadens their minds so."[12] I'm not sure whether Lewis would have considered himself to be a dog or a cat (I suspect the former), but he also had to struggle with the notion of attending unappealing worship services:

> When I first became a Christian about fourteen years ago, I thought that I could do it on my own, by retiring to my room and reading theology and I wouldn't go to churches and Gospel halls . . . I disliked very much their hymns, which I considered to be fifth-rate poems set to sixth-rate music. But as I went I saw the merit of it. I came up against different people of quite different outlooks and different education, and then gradually my conceit just began peeling away. You realize that those sixth-rate hymns are being sung with devotion and benefit by an old saint in elastic-side boots in the opposite pew, and then you realize that *you* aren't fit to clean those boots.[13]

So, if my Austin friend had begun attending the *Ozzie and Harriet* church, maybe his conceit (the self-interest that was the ultimate source of his boredom) would have peeled away. Or maybe he would have been the catalyst for God to peel away the conceit of another, some Lewis-like old dog prone to look down on him because of his dress or taste in music. But even if none of that happened, he'd only be wasting one hour a week worshiping the God who is so good to him—how bad could that be?

"Don't be afraid to waste time with God."
JWC

## Hide and Seek

Why do we go to church? To worship God. And why do we worship God? Because God is wonderful and glorious and worthy of our praise. Worship is an act of love, and that's why we go to church, because we *love* God. All it takes is a little speck of faith, just a mustard seed. That's all. You can come and be bored. You can come and doubt. You can come and complain, gripe all the way home about the pastor and the music and the building and all your fellow worshipers. But search your soul: somewhere within is there not a little speck of faith, a spark of love for the Lord who gives you life?

What if there isn't? Ah, well, then I have some really good news. Such faith is a gift of God: "This is not your own doing," the apostle says, lest "one may boast" (Ephesians 2:8)—and he should know, being a bit of an expert on boasting (2 Corinthians 11:16-33). Here, then, is what you should do: pray to the God you don't believe in, and ask for the love of this God to be shed abroad in your unbelieving heart (Romans 5:5). Ask, search, and knock (Matthew 7:7). It doesn't matter whether you believe it or not. Whoever calls upon the name of the Lord will be saved (Joel 2:32), and if *having faith* were a prerequisite for asking for faith . . . well, that wouldn't make much sense, would it? Pray for the Holy Spirit, for a little speck of faith, for a little spark of love. Then what? I don't know, but if I were you I would drag my speckless, sparkless, Spirit-less self into a church building on a Sunday morning and wait to see what happened. We don't have to find God. According to the Bible, God finds us. Did you ever think that *you* might be the one for whom the ninety-nine are forsaken (Luke 15:3-7)?

When I was a child we used to play hide-and-seek. One person would count backward from one hundred while we all searched for a clever place of concealment. I still remember the exhilaration as the numbers were being called: "ninety-six . . . ninety-five . . . ninety-four . . ." When they got to zero, time would be up. You couldn't say, "Wait, give me another moment." You'd better be hidden really well, or you would be found. Of course, you would be found anyway, eventually—it was just a matter of time. But once I found an exceptionally good spot, and I stayed hidden for what seemed a very long time. What I discovered was that this really wasn't much fun: all by myself, alone, keeping very quiet. That got old fast. I began to wonder why nobody had found me. Maybe they weren't even trying. Maybe everyone had quit and gone off to play some other game without even telling me. Maybe they didn't *care* whether they found me or not. At last, I could stand it no longer and had to poke my head out to see. Then, of course, I got caught and had to be "it," but at least I was back in the game.

Hide-and-seek is sort of an interesting game from a psychological perspective. Everybody hides, but in reality, everybody *wants* to be found. Hiding (alone) isn't much fun, but being *found*—that's exciting. I don't know a lot about what's called "psychology of religion," but I suspect that people sometimes hide from God for just that reason: they want to be found. And I suspect that (brings us back together)

135

when people *say* they don't have faith, often they do, but they are hiding it. I don't mean to suggest that they are dishonest—they may have hidden it from themselves as well. But here is something else that happens on Sunday morning, another reason for going to church: God finds us there. Of course, God can find us anywhere, just as we can love God anywhere, but for some reason, worship is a special time: we love God best when we worship, and it is in worship that God often deigns to find us, to give us faith, or to bring out of hiding the faith that was there all along.

So come to church and worship the Lord. Or come to be found. I can't say when it will happen or where it will happen, but if you call upon the Lord when you come to worship, you can certainly expect *something* to happen sooner or later. Maybe it will be a sermon or a Scripture text or a snippet of liturgy. Maybe it will happen when you receive Communion or join the congregation in prayer or share greetings of peace with those who share your doubts and dreams. Just *knowing* it's going to happen brings excitement to an otherwise drab occasion. It's like hearing those numbers counting down from one hundred. It's like the prophet Isaiah calling, "Prepare the way of the Lord" (Isaiah 40:3). It's like Jesus announcing, "The kingdom of God has come near" (Mark 1:15). It's as if God is about to spin around and shout, "Ready or not, here I come!" And that's exactly what happens. God finds us, always, whether we are ready or not.

And then, *then,* we can worship; then we can love. We can give an hour and a *life* to this God who always finds us. We can praise this Lord who is worthy to be praised, give thanks and adoration to the God who is so good to us. We can waste our time in worship and know that it is time well spent.

> We love God best when we worship, and it is in worship that God often deigns to find us, to give us faith, or to bring out of hiding the faith that was there all along.

# CHAPTER FIFTEEN

# Hearts and Treasures

A woman once asked me, "What can I do to love God more?" It seemed like the kind of question that a pastor ought to be able to answer. We are always telling people that they should "love the Lord with all their heart and soul and mind." And now here was this woman who said, "I don't think I love God as much as I should. What can I do to love God more?" We had not covered this, as such, in seminary, but one thing I did learn there was "when you need an answer, check the Bible." So, I got a concordance and looked up the word *love* and looked for passages that might tell us whether it is possible to love God *more*, and what we might do to help that happen.

I found a story in chapter 7 of Luke's Gospel. A sinful woman comes to Jesus while he is having dinner with Simon the Pharisee. She sits on the floor and weeps and wipes his feet with her hair. Simon gripes about this, so Jesus tells them a parable. He says, imagine that two people owe someone money—one of them a great deal, the other just a little bit. This person tells both debtors, don't worry about paying me back—just forget it. So, which of the two, Jesus asks, will love him *more*? Simon answers, the one who was forgiven more. Even so, the sinful woman in Luke's story shows great love for Jesus because her sins, though many, have been forgiven. Simon, by contrast, has only a pittance of love for Jesus, because he doesn't think he needs much forgiveness. The moral of the story seems to be, "Whoever is forgiven much, loves much" (compare Luke 7:47).

We must be careful not to squeeze too much out of a parable. There is more to love than mere gratitude, and I suspect Jesus would have agreed with The Beatles that love is not something one can purchase. The point, furthermore, is not that Simon needs to get out and sin so that he will be in need of more forgiveness. No, Jesus is indicating that love is relational and that a correct sense of *who we are* and *who God is* allows that relationship to develop as it should. Simon seems to think of God as a rule maker, whose rules he appreciates and keeps. His relationship to God is a business partnership, something like that of employer and employee. The weeping woman has come to know the heart of God. She comes as a sinner to the friend of sinners, and this understanding of *who she is* and *who God is* has allowed her relationship with God to become one of genuine love.

*Through regular confession of sin, we not only own up to who we are, but we also enter into the very heart of God, discovering that God is merciful and kind, that God is love.*

So I told the woman who came to me with her question, try this: confess your sins regularly to God, and give thanks always for your forgiveness. The simple devotional habit of doing this will become a constant reminder of God's grace, and, according to Jesus, the more aware you become of forgiveness, the more your love for God will grow. It's not *just* gratitude, though it is partly that. It is a relationship, and as with any relationship, true love flourishes as the parties come to know each other more intimately. Through regular confession of sin, we not only own up to who we are (a psychologically healthy exercise in its own right), but we also enter into the very heart of God, discovering that God is merciful and kind, that God *is* love. According to Jesus, this is what inspires us to love God much and to love God more.

## God and Mammon

The Bible also says something else about what we can do to love God more. I found this while looking for an answer to the woman's question, but I was too embarrassed to share it with her. In Matthew 6:24, Jesus says, "No one can serve two masters; for a slave will either hate the one and love the other, or be devoted to the one and despise the other." The context here is concern for loving God—not just believing in God or trusting God or having faith in God but *loving* God. And Jesus goes on to say that this is antithetical to loving mammon. What does that mean? *Mammon* means material things, money and the things that money can buy. Jesus says, rather famously, that those who try to love both God and mammon are doomed to fail: they become slaves to mammon, possessed (as it were) by their own possessions.

Again, we must be careful not to go too far with this observation. We should not despise the material world that God has made. We should be grateful to God for jobs and income and clothing and food and all sorts of things that enhance our lives. The world is good (Genesis 1:31), it is God's (Psalm 24:1), and we are meant to enjoy it (Psalm 118:24). But Jesus is on to something here, something that virtually all people know intuitively to be true. Devotion to material things often prevents us from growing spiritually, from growing in our love for God.

It is easy for preachers to work this observation into a message that induces more guilt than hope. But Jesus also says, "Where your treasure is, there your heart will be also" (Matthew 6:21). This, I note, is a promise. It is not a commandment, and it is not just an observation about life: it is *a promise.* Most people seem to get the point backward. They think that Jesus said, "Where your heart is, that's where your treasure will end up." I've heard sermons on this: people spend their money on the things they truly care about. If you look back over your check register, you will see what is most important to you. Do you spend more money on sporting events than on giving to the church? Then, that is where your heart is.

Well, all of this may be true, but it isn't terribly profound, and it also isn't what Jesus said. Jesus did not say, "Where your heart is, there your treasure will be." He said it the other way around: where you put your treasure, that is where your heart will go. It is a promise. According to Jesus, there is a way for us to alter our spiritual affections. We can decide what we want to care about, and then we can do something that will change us inside until we really do care about those things. We can decide who or what we want to love, and then we can do something to direct our hearts accordingly.

> According to Jesus, there is a way for us to alter our spiritual affections. We can decide what we want to care about, and then we can do something that will change us inside until we really do care about those things.

139

Now you can see why I was embarrassed to tell the woman this. As her pastor, I didn't want to say, "If you want to love God more, you should give more money to the church." That would have been pretty crass, though, in retrospect, I have to admit that it may have been biblically correct and true. So, crass or not, I'm telling *you*: there seems to be some kind of causal connection between stewardship and piety, between financial giving and spiritual devotion. Everyone knows the latter can motivate the former. Jesus reveals that it can also work the other way around: what we do with our money affects how deeply and how purely we love our God.

As near as I can tell, "giving from the heart" is unscriptural, though it is a popular concept in churches. Christians urge each other to "give from the heart," indicating that our gifts should be offered with sincerity, not out of some sense of duty. But Jesus does not want us to give from the heart. He wants us to give according to where we believe our hearts *should be*, to give according to where we hope our hearts *will someday be*. Give of your treasure, and let your heart catch up.

Of course, I'm wary of this turning into some kind of scam for fund-raising. There *is* a solid biblical principle that connects spiritual rewards with the renunciation of material things, but preachers—especially those on television—can seize upon this and abuse it. Still, the principle itself remains legitimate. It has nothing to do with fund-raising and everything to do with spiritual growth: there may be no more sure recipe for spiritual growth than giving away your money. There is probably no more *biblical* recipe for spiritual growth than that.

> There may be no more sure recipe for spiritual growth than giving away your money. There is probably no more *biblical* recipe for spiritual growth than that.

Many people do not realize that this is why we have offerings in church in the first place. It's not fund-raising, but an act of worship, to let people free themselves of devotion to mammon and commit their hearts in devotion to God. Originally, the Israelites brought grain offerings. That was their money—sheaves of wheat. They piled these on the altars and they lit them on fire and just burned them up. What was the point of that? Worship. Then, after a little while, somebody said, "Instead of just burning up this wheat we could give it to the poor, or maybe let the priests eat it." That seemed like a good idea, so they did that, and then before long, people began to think that

140

the *reason* they brought the grain offerings was to help the poor or feed the priests. Likewise, people today think that the *reason* they put money in the offering plate on Sunday morning is to help their church pay its bills or support missions and other good projects. That's not it. Your church does need to pay its bills, and it probably does use your money for lots of good causes, but that is not why the church asks you to give the money in the first place.

Every child of God has a spiritual need to take some of his or her material possessions each and every week and *get rid of them.* In a basic sense, it doesn't matter whether the sheaves get burned up or the money gets put to good use or not. You need to put money in that offering plate not because the church needs your money, but because *you need to give it.* Most pastors know this to be true, though they have a hard time talking about it: people who do not give regularly of their money are not healthy spiritually, and people who do not *increase* their giving regularly are not *growing* spiritually. Of course, there are all sorts of caveats and exceptions to this general rule—people who suffer financial setbacks, people who feel moved to give to causes other than their local church, and so on. No one—no minister or anyone else—should ever judge the heart of any individual based on this or any other external standard. There are many other factors involved. I offer this only as a matter for your own conscience, for your personal consideration. As a general rule, if you want to love God more, start giving away more of your money. Where your treasure is, there your heart will be, Jesus said, and it's a promise. Not a requirement, but a promise.

If it seems like I'm meddling in your personal affairs, I'm sorry, but I'm afraid the situation might get even worse as we segue into the next section. I have noticed only one thing that modern Westerners treasure more than their mammon: their *time.* So, of course, the same principle applies. If you want to love Jesus in this complicated . . . no, make that, in this *busy, hectic, over-scheduled,* and *frenzied* world . . . then pry open your precious treasure chest and give him what you value most: your time.

## An Appointment with God

Many people in the Bible are described as regularly taking time to disengage from the mundane and material world about them to focus for a time on matters of spiritual concern. The Bible presents David (Psalm 55:17) and Daniel (Daniel 6:10) and Peter (Acts 10:9) and Paul (2 Timothy 1:3) as individuals who regularly devote time each day to prayer. And, throughout the Gospels, we find that personal, private, and deliberate prayer is also a significant mark of Jesus' relationship with God:

- "After he had dismissed the crowds, he went up on the mountain by himself to pray" (Matthew 14:23).
- "In the morning, while it was still very dark, he got up and went out to a deserted place, and there he prayed" (Mark 1:35).
- "Now during those days he went out to the mountain to pray; and he spent the night in prayer to God" (Luke 6:12).

Likewise, virtually all spiritual leaders throughout the centuries have had this one thing in common: commitment to some sort of personal devotional life. John Wesley is said to have spent two hours a day in prayer, and an associate of Martin Luther reported that "not a day passes during which he does not spend in prayer at least *three* hours."[14] But then (not to be outdone) Wesley claimed with devout irony that when he was especially busy he would increase the time: "I have so much to do that I must spend *many* hours in prayer before I am able to do it."[15] This begins to sound like a horse race, with Lutherans and Wesleyans (not to mention Calvinists and Zwinglians and Mennonites and Franciscans and others whose forbears, we should note, were also renowned for such habits) extolling the saintliness of their namesakes. The point, however, is this: even when we make allowance for pious exaggeration, we cannot deny that some sort of constant spiritual discipline has always marked the lives of people who were thought to be close to God.

What might this mean for *us*—people who want to love Jesus and be closer to God, but who live in a very complicated world? You know, of course, that there are people in this world who still do things like this. There are religious people (including Christians) who practice various forms of meditation. You may have heard about people (and not just monks) who keep disciplines of fasting or silence or solitude or celibacy in order to heighten their spiritual consciousness. You might know people who burn candles or pray rosaries or who simply read their Bibles every morning or kneel by their beds every night. If you have trouble imagining that you could ever be such a person, try focusing on the larger theme of simply offering to God the gift of your time. What, precisely, you do with that time is of secondary importance. If you want to just sit there and do nothing, fine. Actually, there's pretty good precedent for that (Psalm 46:10). The main point is to take this treasure that seeks to own you and place it where you want your heart to be. Give this time to God, and your heart will follow.

We are speaking of premeditated contact with the divine that is both intense and intentional, of keeping an appointment with God, so to speak. Some people will say, God is everywhere, and I can experience God's presence at any time. Yes, but do you? I don't doubt that it is possible to attain a level of spiritual awareness that allows mere mortals to experience God as active and present in every instance of their lives. There are saints who testify to this. Still, I personally relate more readily to the words of that pilgrim, John Bunyan, who lamented, "None know how many bye-ways and back lanes the heart hath to slip away from the presence of God."[16] What we need, I think, is to create a space and time that is set apart for noticing the presence of God in our lives. That's the point. God is with us everywhere and always—but we don't *notice*. acknowledge God's presence—awareness.

No matter how old-fashioned or outmoded the concept of "personal devotions" might seem, people who want to be closer to God need to have some kind of strategy for connecting with God in a deliberate way, for noticing God's presence in a way that they would not notice otherwise. One of the great spiritual leaders of our time, Henri Nouwen, says flatly that "a spiritual life without discipline is impossible,"[17] and by *discipline* he means the practice of setting aside time on a regular basis to focus very intentionally on our relationship with God. I don't really like the word *discipline*, because it sounds like a synonym for *punishment*. But Nouwen's point is that a choice is necessary, and a commitment is required. This is not something that will "just happen" unless we act to make it happen.

> What I want to encourage you to do is to take time each day to be alone with God, to think about God, to tell God whatever is on your heart, and to give God an opportunity to speak to you.

What I want to encourage you to do is to take time each day to be alone with God, to think about God, to tell God whatever is on your heart, and to give God an opportunity to speak to you. Jesus said, "Go into your room and shut the door and pray to your Father who is in secret" (Matthew 6:6). We need to commit ourselves to do this (the *discipline* part) because, even though human beings are creatures of habit, they are not naturally prone to develop habits that provide for their *spiritual* needs. As for the specifics, I think that it is generally best if you can use the same time and place every day, but the

make it an enjoyable
Routine, like eating, sleeping, or
Spending time with friend, Routine you love are enjoyable.

details of *when* and *where* are not ultimately important and may be crafted to meet your own schedule and preferences. Many people find that mornings are best, to help them "get a start on the day." On the other hand, mornings can be harried and hectic times, and you may end up trying to pray with one eye on the clock. So to avoid *that* problem (you'll still encounter others), evenings might work better. In any case, most people who do this try to find a space—a "prayer closet"—in their home and, if need be, they tell family members that they are not to be disturbed during their devotional time. Even then, distractions can intrude—it is hard to stay spiritually focused when you can hear the kids fighting downstairs. Some people choose a time when no one else is home or find a location outside the home where they will have more privacy. Go out to the garage and commune with God among the rakes and paint cans. Thomas Merton suggests that city dwellers drop into one of those big cathedrals they pass on the way to work and find a dark corner all to themselves. The ugly churches are best, he says, because they get the fewest visitors.[18] But if you lack such options, just make the best of things and try to *use* the distractions rather than being distracted by them: when the kids start fighting, pray for *them*.

How much time are we talking about? I don't know—how much can you afford? If you want me to decide for you, I'll say "thirty minutes a day," just as a suggestion. Try that, and see what happens. Again, personally, I like to take the time all at once—devote a half-hour slot to spiritual devotions—but I know people who prefer to split up the time—ten minutes in the morning, ten minutes at noon, ten minutes at night. Whatever you do, don't beat yourself up when you are unable to keep to the regimen. Most of us don't need *more* things in our lives to make us feel guilty or inadequate, and your devotional life should never become an occasion for nurturing such feelings. If you commit yourself to spending a half-hour each day and only do it three times a week, that's a lot better than not committing yourself at all and doing it zero times a week.

## In Praise of Duty

You may be excused for thinking that this chapter has been about all sorts of things: ritual confession of sins, stewardship of personal finances, and the development of devotional habits. In my mind there is a common theme, which I had best make explicit: spiritual devotion is a matter of duty. For me, learning this has been one more point in the development of a second naïveté (see page 12). At an earlier point in my life, a time that I would now regard as spiritual immaturity, I connected true spirituality with *sincerity* and disparaged ritual acts that might entail "just going through the motions." There is, of course, something to such a denunciation, and I still prize heartfelt sincerity as important to cultivation of the spiritual life. But I have discovered that there is some value in those motions that one may sometimes be "just going through." The heart, Jesus indicates, can sometimes be affected by decisions we make about such mundane matters as what we do with our basic resources: our money and our time. Developing true piety, that is, a genuine spiritual devotion to God, depends upon being faithful in certain matters whether we feel like it or not. What we said about participating in Sunday worship in the last chapter applies also to the matters we have just discussed in this one. We worship God, we confess our sins, we offer God a generous share of all that we treasure, not necessarily because we feel moved to do so, but because such actions are called for. They are called for by the mere fact of *who God is* and *who we are.* Ideally, of course, our duty becomes our delight. In my experience, this does happen, but it doesn't always happen immediately or predictably. Every spiritual journey is filled with surprises, and spiritual commitments merely put us on various roads to discovery.

## MAKING TIME FOR GOD

*Before our daily bread should be our daily Word.*
*Before our daily work should be our daily prayer.*
*Before the heart unlocks itself for the world, God wants to open it for himself.*
*Before the ear takes in the countless voices of the day, it should hear in the early hours the voice of the Creator and Redeemer.*
*God prepared the stillness of the first morning for himself. It should remain his.*

Dietrich Bonhoeffer

*There should be at least a room, or some corner where no one will find you and disturb you or notice you. You should untether yourself from the world and set yourself free, loosing all the strings and strands of tension that bind you by sight, by sound, by thought, to the presence of others.*

Thomas Merton

*It is a good thing to let prayer be the first business of the morning and the last of the evening. Guard yourself carefully against such false and deceitful thoughts that keep whispering, 'Wait awhile. In an hour or so I will pray. I must finish this or that.' Thinking such thoughts we get away from prayer into business, until the day has come to nought.*

Martin Luther (in a personal letter to his barber)

*We should pray when we are in a praying mood, for it would be sinful to neglect so fair an opportunity. We should pray when we are not in a praying mood because it would be dangerous to remain in so unhealthy a condition.*

Charles Spurgeon

# CHAPTER SIXTEEN

# Something to Savor

Many biblical writers compare the word of God to food. Moses said, "One does not live by bread alone, but by every word that comes from the mouth of the Lord" (Deuteronomy 8:3). Well, obviously, people need more than bread. They need at least three other food groups: dairy and meat and vegetables. But, curiously, the word of God is not usually compared to such healthy choices. More often, it is likened to *honey*, which goes on the bread to make it sweet (see Psalm 19:10; Ezekiel 3:3; Jeremiah 15:16).

Most people today probably don't think of the Bible as something *delicious*. They can't imagine ever coming to regard devotional Bible reading as their dessert. They might think that developing such a discipline is something they should do, something that would be good for them, but they do not expect it ever to become something they would do for the sheer joy of it. A duty, perhaps, but not a delight.

So this chapter is going to be about reading the Bible. I don't know what your experience with Bible reading has been up to now, and I can't guarantee that if you take up the habit it will bring you the kind of pleasure that it has sometimes brought to others. There's honey in this book, but there are some bitter pills to swallow too. I think I can promise you this: if you read the Bible regularly with an openness to receiving God's word, you will grow spiritually.

and come closer to God. Also, for what it's worth, the practice of *devotional* Bible reading focuses without apology on finding what will be of most value to you, personally. You may be asked to taste lots of things, but the goal is to find something to savor.

When we use the Bible for personal devotions, we use it in a way that was never intended. With very few exceptions, the books of the Bible were originally addressed to communities, not individuals, and the Bible remains the word of God to Israel and to the whole Christian church, not to us alone. The meaning of the Bible always transcends personal application, and if we really want to understand the Scriptures we need to grapple with what they have to say to

> If you read the Bible regularly with an openness to receiving God's word, you will grow spiritually and come closer to God.

the *communities* of which we are a part: our family, our church, our nation, our species. Nevertheless, saints and pilgrims throughout the ages have testified to the powerful reality of coming closer to God through personal, devotional Bible reading. The dangerous flip side of thinking "It's all about me" is thinking "It's never about me." If you want to avoid both pitfalls, a discipline of devotional Bible reading may help you to recognize what God has to say to you, specifically, at any particular point in your life.

---

**SCRIPTURE ON SCRIPTURE:**
**WHAT THE BIBLE SAYS ABOUT THE WORD OF GOD**

- "One does not live by bread alone, but by every word that comes from the mouth of the Lord" (Deuteronomy 8:3; Matthew 4:4).

- "(God says) So shall my word be that goes out from my mouth; it shall not return to me empty, but it shall accomplish that which I purpose, and succeed in the thing for which I sent it" (Isaiah 55:11).

- "All Scripture is inspired by God and is useful for teaching, for reproof, for correction, and for training in righteousness" (2 Timothy 3:16).

- "The word of God is living and active, sharper than any two-edged sword, piercing until it divides soul from spirit, joints from marrow; it is able to judge the thoughts and intentions of the heart" (Hebrews 4:12).

- "Be doers of the word, and not merely hearers who deceive themselves" (James 1:22).

# A Living Word

Many people worry that if they read the Bible on their own—that is, without a teacher—they will not be able to understand it. If they know nothing else about the Bible, they know that it is a big book that is often difficult to understand. But devotional Bible reading is not the same thing as Bible *study*. The goal is not to arrive at a theologically or doctrinally correct interpretation of the text (though that is never a bad thing to do); the goal is to engage the Scripture in a way that we would rarely engage any other writing, to understand what was written in these ancient books as God's words to *us* and to respond to them in just that way. The teacher is the Holy Spirit, who Jesus promised would reveal the things of God to us and lead us into all truth (John 16:13).

I do not mean by this that God speaks to us directly or magically through the Bible, as though it were a collection of horoscopes, fortune cookies, or Tarot cards. There are Christians who view the Bible that way, and when I was younger I may have been among them. I once knew a woman who told me that she began every day by reading a passage from the Bible to find out what God wanted her to do. For instance, when she read Isaiah 55:1 ("Come, buy wine and milk"), she took this to mean that God wanted her to go grocery shopping. I think this is at best silly, and at worst dangerous. There is an old preachers' joke about such a person, a man who just happened to open the Bible to the verse that says, "Judas went out and hanged himself." Unsure what that might mean for him, he closed the book and opened it again to read, "Go thou and do likewise." So much for dangerous. As for silly, Erick Nelson remembers someone who opened the Bible to Isaiah 55:12 ("you shall go out with joy," RSV) and determined that God wanted him to date a girl named Joy. No report on how that turned out.

But the Bible *does* speak God's living Word to us. A woman once told me that she read Galatians 5:15 for her morning devotions and felt convicted by God to call her sister and try to make amends for the animosity between them. That text says, "If, however, you bite and devour one another, take care that you are not consumed by one another." Paul did not write that passage with this woman in mind. He wrote it 1,900 years before she was born, out of a concern for strained relationships between Jews and Gentiles in a congregation struggling with the ramifications of cross-cultural evangelism. No matter. This woman read Paul's ancient words *devotionally,* and God spoke to her in a manner that Paul himself might not have anticipated.

In reading the Bible, we always want to pay attention to two contexts: the historical context in which the passage was first written, and the present context in which we now live. Theological Bible study emphasizes the first, but should not completely ignore the latter; devotional Bible reading emphasizes the latter, but should not completely ignore the first. Biblical commentaries and other study aids are now widely available to supply us with information about any passage's historical context. Since the Bible was written hundreds of years ago in a culture quite different from our own, we all need help of this sort. If you don't know what the *Urim and Thummim* were or what a *phylactery* is, you may have trouble understanding some biblical texts at a basic level. Still, the focus of devotional Bible reading is personal application. It is easy, especially for the academically inclined, to get sidetracked by all sorts of interesting historical concerns that prevent us from hearing the text as God's Word to *us*.

A Puritan preacher by the name of Thomas Watson used to direct his charges to read the Bible with this attitude: "Take every word as spoken to yourselves. When the word thunders against sin, think thus: 'God means my sins'; when it presseth any duty, 'God intends me in this.'"[19] Well, I think that might be going a bit far. Sometimes the Bible thunders against sins I have never been tempted to commit (child sacrifice) and presses duties that God probably does not want me to perform (killing Philistines). But I get what Watson means, and I think that those who possess a modicum of common sense can probably apply his advice most of the time. If we read with *some* recognition of historical context, we will be able to draw personal applications from the text without always knowing all the details.

Dietrich Bonhoeffer was one of the greatest theologians of the twentieth century, and he surely knew how to study the Bible in intellectual and academic ways. But when he encouraged his students to have personal devotions, he offered this advice: "Just as you do not analyze the words of someone you love, but accept them as they are said to you, so accept the word of Scripture and ponder it in your heart, as Mary did" (see Luke 2:19, 51).[20] That's the type of understanding we are after—not intellectual analysis but an experiential understanding characterized by accepting what the Bible says and pondering it in our hearts.

When I read the Bible devotionally, I focus not on the message that the author wanted to convey to some original audience, but on the *effect* or *impact* that what I am reading has on me today. Sometimes, I discern a message or moral or some sort of lesson that I want to apply to my life, or that I at least

11/05/07   11:44   6       5       8119

Customer Account Record # 0012132213
Charge to Account # C649228

PRICETOWN UNITED METH CHURCH
4640 PRITCHARD OHLTOWN RD
ATTN:TREASURER
NEWTON FALLS, OH 44444-9711
Telephone # (330) 872-3801

ORDERED BY JEFF COGGINS

    1@  17.00  9780800636760 %0$    17.00*
                LOVING JESUS
    1@   5.75 SHIP          %0$     5.75*
SUBTOTAL                     $      22.75
TAX       @ 6.0000%          $       0.00
TOTAL                        $      22.75
TENDERED Charge  0012132213  $      22.75

        This is your invoice.
Please retain to match w/your statement.

x _____phney/mb_____

    MANY BOOKS AND GIFT ITEMS - 50% OFF!!
        TOLL FREE 1-800-830-9516

want to think about more deeply. Other times, the effect is more emotional, even sentimental: I don't necessarily *learn* anything from the text; I just experience its influence and power. Perhaps it inspires me to worship; perhaps it challenges me to repent. Maybe I empathize with one of the characters in a story and feel happy or sad or frightened or confused by their experience with God. I think that people need to know *something* about the historical context for this to work, but not a lot. So, I would suggest, make the best of reading the text that is before you, and maybe write down a few notes about things that you want to check on later. Call your pastor later in the day, and ask him or her about whatever you didn't get at the time. Don't do this every day, however.

# A House on Rock

The key to devotional Bible reading seems to be approaching Scripture with an *expectation* that we will encounter God there and discover God's living Word to us. With that in mind, I want to pass along a few tips that I have accumulated over the years—a few practical ideas that might make your experience with the Bible more rewarding.

*Have a plan.* Devotional Bible reading is a discipline, which means we need to commit to doing it in a way that will be intentional. Decide *when* and *where* you are going to read the Bible—don't just stick one in your car or purse or briefcase to read "when you get a chance." Decide what part of the Bible you're going to read. The best idea will not necessarily be to start at the beginning and just plow through to the end. Many have tried that approach and failed, bogging down in material that is difficult or frustrating and never getting to what they might have found more enriching. You may do better to sample different types of literature: one Old Testament history book, then one of the Gospels, then some poetry or an epistle or one of the prophets. Whatever you start out doing, feel free to alter your habits as you go along. If the time or place isn't working, change it. If you find that reading a particular book is pure drudgery, give it up and read something else. And don't feel guilty about skimming sections that you find incomprehensible or irrelevant, either. This

> The key to devotional Bible reading seems to be approaching Scripture with an expectation that we will *encounter* God there and discover God's living Word to us.

is the wonderful thing about personal devotions: they are *personal,* and you can do whatever you want to do.

*Pray.* Back in the days of the Jesus movement revival, those of us who were called "Jesus freaks" all had cheap paperback Bibles on which we had written P.B.O. in bold letters with cheap felt-tip markers. The letters stood for Pray Before Opening, and we took that seriously. To this day, one of my more important tips for devotional Bible reading is a simple one: begin with prayer. If you're liturgically inclined, you can find prayers for this purpose in various books or hymnals. Otherwise, you can just make one up: "I thank you, God, that the very same Holy Spirit who first inspired these words to be written is here with me now as I read them. Open my heart and my mind to your Word that I may meet you there and hear you speak to me." Something like that.

*Reflect.* One approach to devotions is to read as much of the Bible as possible, perhaps several chapters at a single sitting. The disadvantage, then, is that you may not have much time to reflect meaningfully on what you have read. Another approach is to take a small amount of text, even a single verse, and allow this to inspire and guide you in meditation and prayer. But then you are giving up time with the Bible itself. My advice is not "split the difference," but "don't do it the same way every time." Vary the amount of time apportioned to reading and reflection. For example, if you wish to use Paul's letter to the Romans for your devotions, you might set aside an hour one day to read the entire letter straight through. Then, you might take several days to read through the letter more slowly, perhaps one chapter at a time, highlighting or underlining verses that jump out at you. Then, you might go through the letter a third time, taking for each day a verse that you have marked, thinking deeply about it, and writing in a journal or stating out loud to God what you think the implications of that verse might be for your personal life. The box at the close of this chapter suggests some specific strategies for reflecting on Scripture texts.

*Respond.* Our devotions should be a time for dialogue with God. We listen to what God has to say to us and respond by speaking to God in words of confession, prayer, praise . . . or even argument. Many Christians practice a discipline called "Praying the Text": this means reading through the passage very slowly, one line at a time, thinking about each phrase and then converting your thoughts into prayers. Tell God what you think and how you feel about everything you read.

As a bridge to life in the real world, many Christians like to memorize Bible passages that are especially meaningful or helpful to them. I know this sounds tedious—it probably brings back scary memories of studying for tests in school. You also might have known some annoying people who have memorized Bible verses and like to quote them (chapter and verse) for the unsolicited enlightenment of those who they think will benefit from their efforts. Well, it doesn't have to be like that: think of it more as treasuring God's Word in your heart, keeping it with you so that you can reflect on it more deeply at will (see Psalm 119:11). Anthony Bloom, a Russian Orthodox Archbishop, says, "Learn those passages, because one day when you are completely low, so profoundly desperate that you cannot call out of your soul any spontaneous expression, you will discover that these words come up and offer themselves to you as a gift of God, as a gift of the Church."[21]

Eventually, the effectiveness of your time spent reading the Bible will be determined by the effect that this time has on the rest of your life. This point seems sufficiently obvious that I do not feel compelled to belabor it. Only hear what the brother of our Lord says: "Be *doers of the word*, and not merely hearers who deceive themselves" (James 1:22; italics mine). And recall the parable Jesus tells at the conclusion of his Sermon on the Mount: "Everyone then who hears these words of mine and *acts on them* will be like a wise man who built his house on rock" (Matthew 7:24; italics mine). Or, let's put it this way: the whole purpose of reading the Bible devotionally is to come closer to God by learning to love Jesus in this complicated world. And this Jesus whom we seek to love tells us, "Those who love me will keep my word" (John 14:23).

## Believing the Bible

What does it mean to *believe* the Bible? It seems to mean different things to different people. All Christians say the Bible is the word of God and that it is inspired by God, but some Christians also say that it is "inerrant," and lots of Christians get in arguments over whether or not there are any contradictions in the Bible and whether what the Bible says is *literally* true or just true in some other sense. I suppose these discussions are important for various theological reasons, but they may not be *as* important when we want to read the Bible devotionally as a means for growing closer to God. The goal is to engage Scripture at a heartfelt level that speaks specifically to us.

In fact, I think that just about the surest way to miss out on what God has to offer you through Scripture is to allow your experience of devotional Bible reading to get derailed by these kinds of concerns. The point of spiritual

153

devotions is neither to defend the Bible nor to investigate the extent to which it is accurate or reliable or true, but to accept it in some basic sense as God's word and allow it to reveal what God wants to say to us. In this regard, I will also say that we should not be trying to read the Bible as a book about science or geography or history but as a book about God. For devotional purposes, at least, we are only interested in what the Bible has to say about God and about us and about God's relationship with us. The question of whether the Bible is accurate in what it says about all kinds of other topics may be interesting and worthy of pursuit by the intellectually curious, but that question has little to do with appreciating the Bible's primary function of drawing us closer to God.

Still, the practical problem that arises for well-meaning Bible readers is this: What do I do when I cannot personally accept what the Bible says? The "touch points" will be different for different people. Someone will read about the miracle of the virgin birth (Matthew 1:18-25) and think, "Well, I just don't believe that happened." Someone else will read the parenting advice in Proverbs 13:24 or Paul's counsel to wives in Ephesians 5:22 and be appalled: "I don't agree with this! I think the Bible is wrong!" What should you do when this happens? Say so. Tell God, "I don't think I agree with this—I don't think I believe it—am I missing something?" And then move on. Maybe someday you'll come to understand it differently; maybe your mind will change, or maybe not. There's little point in *pretending*, at any rate. God already knows your heart (your beliefs, your doubts, your biases, your fears), and there's nobody else around to impress. So, read what the Bible says and tell God what you think and how you feel about what you read. Tell God how it *affects* you, regardless of what the intended message might be. Accept the Bible's invitation to engage the God of Scripture, and do this in a way that is honest and vulnerable.

And this is the most important thing of all: for Christians, the God of the Bible is also the God who becomes real to us in Jesus Christ. The New Testament declares that Jesus himself is the ultimate Word of God (John 1:1). In most liturgical churches, when the Gospel lesson is read on Sunday morning, the entire congregation responds by shouting or singing, "Praise to you, O Christ!" They do not say, "Praise to you, O Bible!" and there is a reason for that. We do not worship the Bible because the Bible does not love us, and we cannot have a relationship with the Bible. Jesus does love us, and we can have a relationship with him. The Bible, then, is the Word of God, but it is also a *means to an end*. For Christians, everything is a means to an end, except Jesus Christ. Knowing Jesus and being known by him, loving Jesus and being loved by him—*that* is what counts. For Christians, that is what being close to God means. Therefore, we read everything in the Bible from a particular perspective: *What does this mean for people who are in a relationship with God through Jesus Christ?* Eventually, everything in the Bible (yes, even the Old Testament) helps us to know Jesus Christ and to love Jesus Christ and to have a relationship with Jesus Christ, who is risen from the dead.

## A Two-Edged Sword

What can you expect if you adopt the discipline of regular devotional Bible reading? Thomas Merton says, "It is the nature of the Bible to affront, perplex, and astonish the human mind. Hence the reader who opens the Bible must be prepared for disorientation, confusion, incomprehension, perhaps outrage."[22] If the Bible truly is the Word of God, and we are mere mortals, how could this be otherwise? The Bible tells us of God's thoughts and ways, and God's thoughts are not our thoughts, and God's ways are not our ways (Isaiah 55:8).

So, what can you expect? Well, you will learn a lot of Bible content and probably discover that the Bible says a lot of things and tells a lot of stories that you had no idea were in there—things that didn't make the lectionary and that never get mentioned in church. Much of this is pretty interesting— but that isn't really the point. You'll also be bored sometimes, frustrated, maybe even outraged in the sense that Merton describes. But then there will be searing moments when the Bible speaks straight to your heart, and you will wonder how this ancient writer could possibly have known you so well. "The word of God is living and active," the letter to the Hebrews says, "sharper than any two-edged sword, piercing until it divides soul from spirit, joints from marrow; it is able to judge the thoughts and intentions of the heart" (Hebrews 4:12). I guess that doesn't sound too pleasant either. But there will be other times—I hope *frequent* times—when the Bible will speak words of comfort and blessing and healing that surpass anything that any human friend might have offered. You should hear all these words, the painful and the pleasant, the bitter and the sweet, as a personal communication from God to you. Above all, if you begin a regular practice of devotional Bible reading, you will be drawn closer to God. I have known dozens, indeed hundreds, of persons who have done so, and have never known a one to say that this was not true.

We'll close this chapter with some words from Geoffrey Thomas, one of many experienced pilgrims who have made this discovery:

155

Do not expect to master the Bible in a day, or a month, or a year. Rather, expect often to be puzzled by its contents . . . Do not expect always to get an emotional charge or a feeling of quiet peace when you read the Bible . . . often, you will get no emotional response at all. But let the Word break over your heart and mind again and again as the years go by, and imperceptibly there will come great changes in your attitude and outlook and conduct. You will probably be the last to recognize these. Often you will feel very, very small, because increasingly the God of the Bible will become to you wonderfully great. So go on reading it until you can read no longer, and then you will not need the Bible any more, because when your eyes close for the last time in death, and never again read the Word of God in Scripture, you will open them to the Word of God in the flesh, that same Jesus of the Bible whom you have known for so long, standing before you to take you for ever to his eternal home.[23]

---

### REFLECTING ON SCRIPTURE:
### HOW TO FIND PERSONAL MEANING IN BIBLE TEXTS

#### *Compare Different Versions*
Read the same Bible text in several different English translations, noticing the different connotations that they offer.

#### *Ask Questions for Personal Application*
Read the passage and ask questions like these (suggested by Donald Whitney):
- Does this text reveal something I should believe about God?
- Does this text reveal something I should praise or thank or trust God for?
- Does this text reveal something I should pray about for myself or others?
- Does this text reveal something I should have a new attitude about?
- Does this text reveal something I should make a decision about?
- Does this text reveal something I should do for the sake of Christ, others, or myself?

Another pattern (suggested by David Mann): Does this passage reveal a
- Sin to confess?
- Promise to believe?
- Example to follow?
- Command to obey?
- Knowledge to gain?

And remember to look for this "speck" in your *own* eye (Matthew 7:3).

**Empathize with Characters**

Read a Bible story repeatedly, pretending that you are a different character each time and sensing what you think and how you feel about what transpires. For example, read the story of the prodigal son from the perspective of the prodigal, the father, and the older brother.

**Paraphrase the Passage**

Read a Bible passage and then summarize or rewrite it in your own words. Then compare your paraphrase with the original, noting what you might have added, left out, or changed.

**Emphasize Different Words**

Read a verse repeatedly, putting the stress on different words and thinking about how this brings out different dimensions of the meaning: "For *God* so loved the world"; "For God so *loved* the world"; "For God so loved the *world*."

**Check Cross-References**

Use a study Bible to note where you can find other passages in the Bible similar to one that has struck you (usually listed in the margins or at the bottom of the page). Or, use a concordance to find other verses that use one of the key words in your text.

# CHAPTER SEVENTEEN

# Conversation with God

Many people have told me that, apart from scheduling difficulties, the *real* reason they do not keep a regular devotional life is that they simply don't know how to pray: "Even if I could find the time to pray, say for ten to fifteen minutes a day, I wouldn't know what to say." People may know a couple of prayers that they can say at bedtime or before a meal, but they don't always know how to make up prayers on their own—certainly not enough to fill more than a minute or two of time.

If this is you, do not be embarrassed. Jesus' own disciples did not know how to pray either. They were adult men who had apparently been pretty religious all their lives when they came to him and said, "Lord, teach us to pray, as John taught his disciples" (Luke 11:1)—I guess this means that John's disciples didn't know how to pray either. In any case, I will try in this chapter to describe a simple way to pray that is easy to learn and that should enable you to get by until you can branch out on your own and learn other ways. But first, let's just reflect on what prayer is.

"Prayer is conversation with God," the second-century theologian Clement of Alexandria once said (*Stromateis*, 7)—so famously that few would remember it was he who said it first. Was he merely stating the obvious? He also described prayer as keeping "happy company with God," an expression that I think sounds more like something Mister Rogers or Big Bird would have said. The kindergarten connotation could be appropriate. Clement would have us begin by thinking of prayer as *play,* not work. It *can* be work, of course (Luther called prayer "the sweat of the soul"), but at least initially our goal will not be to exorcize demons (Mark 9:29) or transplant mulberry trees (Luke 17:6). Let prayer be recess, not craft time, gym, or study hall. And let it be "conversation with God": prayer is simply talking with God and expressing our thoughts, feelings, and desires in an honest and vulnerable way. It is also listening to God, which means that sometimes it is all right not to say anything at all. But when we do talk to God, we ought not feel any compulsion to speak in a proper or dignified manner. Jesus encourages us to pray to God as a child would speak to a loving parent. This means that it is all right for our prayers to be somewhat childish—it is all right to say things that are silly or wrong. No loving parents would want their child to be reluctant to talk to them for fear of not using the right words or saying the right thing. This, of course, is another reason for praying in private. You don't have to worry about what anyone else might think of your prayers. Pray to God "in secret," Jesus says (Matthew 6:6). Just tell God what you think and how you feel.

> Prayer is simply talking with God and expressing our thoughts, feelings, and desires in an honest and vulnerable way. It is also listening to God.

## Postures for Prayer

We're going to talk about "what to say," but first, let's think about what to do. Is there an appropriate posture for prayer? No. The Bible portrays Abraham as "standing before the Lord" to pray (Genesis 18:22), David as seated (2 Samuel 7:18-29), a psalmist as lying in bed (Psalm 63:5-6), and Jesus as prostrating himself facedown in the dirt (Mark 14:35). People kneel (Acts 9:40), and bow (Genesis 24:52), and are encouraged to do both (Psalm 95:6-7).

What do they do with their hands? In the Bible, people often pray with their hands uplifted (Psalm 28:2; 63:4; 134:2; 141:2; 1 Timothy 2:8). Curiously, no one in the Bible ever prays with their hands folded, though there is certainly nothing wrong with doing that. Today, some Christians like to pray with their arms folded across their chest as a symbol of humility or with their hands open in their lap as a sign of receptivity. I also like an exercise suggested by Richard Foster:

> Begin by placing your palms down as a symbolic indication of your desire to turn over any concerns you may have to God. Inwardly, you may pray, "Lord, I give you my anger toward John. I release my fear of my dentist appointment. . . ." After several moments of surrender, turn your palms up as a symbol of your desire to receive from the Lord. Perhaps you will pray silently: "Lord, I would like to receive your divine love for John, your peace about the dentist appointment."[24]

The overall point is to use body language to offer our whole self to God as "a living sacrifice" (Romans 12:1), praying with our posture and movements and gestures as well as with our thoughts and words. There is no divinely ordained or theologically correct way to do this. Many people (not just Roman Catholics) like to make the sign of the cross over their body when they begin or conclude a prayer in the name of the Father, Son, and Holy Spirit. St. Dominic (after whom the Dominican order is named) sometimes liked to pray standing on his tiptoes, extending his clasped hands toward heaven so that his entire body took on the shape of an arrow waiting to be shot in the air. At other times he would open his hands above his head to make his body resemble a chalice waiting to be filled. And sometimes he would pray gazing heavenward with his arms spread wide, as if ready to catch some blessing that might fall from the sky. Sounds like a fun guy. You get the point: Experiment. Enjoy.

## A Pattern for Prayer

And, now, here is a very simple model for saying prayers. It has been used for years and those of you who read books on spiritual guidance may have seen it a dozen times before. There's a reason for that: it works. The model suggests a pattern for prayer based on four words that spell out the acronym A-C-T-S:

**A**—Adoration
**C**—Confession
**T**—Thanksgiving
**S**—Supplication

Personally, I wish they were simpler words, not big, religious-sounding ones. I've heard another version of the paradigm called "the four As": Adore, Admit, Appreciate, Ask. I also have a friend who teaches his children to pray by saying, "You're Wonderful, I'm Sorry, Thank You, and Please." But someone taught me the A-C-T-S pattern when I was a child and told me what the big words meant, and it's worked for me ever since.

There are other types of prayer not covered in this little model. There is, for example, the prayer of *lamentation*, where you are just utterly distressed and possibly disappointed with God and want to complain about how things are going. This is not part of the A-C-T-S paradigm because, ideally, it won't have to be a part of your daily routine—but it is very biblical. "Evening and morning and at noon I utter my complaint and moan," one psalmist says (Psalm 55:17). Wow, three times a day! "How long, O Lord?," says another. "Will you forget me forever? How long will you hide your face from me?" (Psalm 13:1). And the author of Psalm 88 is just plain whiny, blaming God for all his problems: "You have caused my companions to shun me" (Psalm 88:8). Such prayers may sound irreverent, but they can serve as an honest act of cleansing and sustain our relationship with God in difficult or troubled times. If you are mad at God, don't hesitate to say so, but say it to God, not just to others.

Right now, though, we want to focus on what I hope could become a more typical pattern for praying. The box on page 164 gives some examples of prayers that follow the A-C-T-S pattern. These are simple prayers, where each portion of the pattern is expressed in a single line. These are the type of prayers that one can say anytime, anywhere. But it is also possible to expand every component of the model. There is plenty to pray about and it is easy to spend ten or fifteen minutes on adoration or confession or thanksgiving or supplication *alone*. As you grow in prayer, you may need to become more comfortable and confident in your conversation with God, but you will soon discover that lack of *material* is not a problem.

**Adoration** (Deuteronomy 6:5; Psalm 29:2; 51:15; John 4:23; Hebrews 13:15). Adoration consists of simply speaking to God of your devotion and love (or maybe singing hymns or other worshipful songs that express those thoughts). Adoration is the essence of worship, praising God not just for what God has done, but for *who God is*. Evelyn Underhill says that adoration is "more deeply refreshing, pacifying, and assuring than any other type of prayer, able to conquer our persistent self-occupation, to expand our spirits, to feed and quicken our awareness of the wonder and delightfulness of God."[25]

Adoration is *recognizing God*, realizing whom we are addressing, and acknowledging this before we say anything else. Jesus began the Lord's Prayer with the words, "Our Father who art in heaven, hallowed be thy name." When the apostles were persecuted and cried out to God for help, they began their prayer by saying, "Sovereign Lord, who made the heaven and the earth, the sea, and everything in them . . ." (Acts 4:24). They made it clear that they knew to whom they were speaking. To help you pray this way, you might actually make a list of God's attributes (powerful, loving, faithful, merciful, kind, unchanging, generous) or make a list of names and titles that you find especially meaningful (Beautiful Savior, Almighty Father, Creator of the Universe, Lord of Earth and Stars). Just start with whatever meager suggestions your imagination supplies, and then, as time goes by, add to your lists (and to your prayers) expressions that you encounter in Scripture or liturgy and wish to make your own.

Confession (Psalm 51:1-12; Luke 18:9-14; 1 John 1:8-9). Confession is the flip side of adoration—it consists of *recognizing who we are*, mortal beings who dare to address the Almighty God, and yet who do so at God's invitation and, so, with full confidence. A prayer of confession is not simply "confession of sin" but of sinfulness, indeed, of humanity. Henri Nouwen says, "To pray is to walk in the full light of God, and to say simply, without holding back, 'I am human and you are God.'" This goes further than mere confession of sins, for "A human being is not someone who once in a while makes a mistake, and God is not someone who now and then forgives. No, human beings *are* sinners and God *is* love."[26] Likewise, confession might involve recognition of our helplessness, an awareness that is liberating when juxtaposed with adoration of a helpful and sustaining God. Ole Hallesby says, "Prayer consists simply in telling God day by day in what ways we find that we are helpless."[27] Nouwen suggests that we might sometimes pray, "I don't know the answer and I can't do this thing, but I don't *have* to know it, and I don't *have* to be able to do it."[28]

Following such basic acknowledgment of humanness, you might also want to go into detail confessing your sins, listing the ways that you think you have failed to be the person you ought to be. I have already spoken of the spiritual benefits of such confession in another chapter (see pages 137–38), but let me note now something that Huckleberry Finn says in the famous novel by Mark Twain: "You can't pray a lie—I found that out." What Huck means is, when we are talking to God in private, all of the excuses and explanations that we might use to rationalize our behavior suddenly sound very silly. We know that God *knows,* so we might as well be honest.

Confession leads rather naturally to repentance and transformation. Simply put, becoming aware of our failings and acknowledging these before God helps us to become better people. C. S. Lewis notes with irony that when humans are becoming better people they are often increasingly aware of their faults, but when they are getting worse they seem to grow ever more oblivious to what everyone else might see.[29] Regular confession of sin prevents us from falling victim to that sort of foolishness and also provides the best-known defense against that fount of vices, self-righteousness. Those who do not regularly confess their sins inevitably tend to think that they are better than other people, whose inadequacies they have somehow not failed to notice (see Luke 18:9-14). And regular confession not only reminds us of our sinfulness but also fosters constant awareness of our absolution, that is, of the "forgiven" status we enjoy as a result of God's mercy and compassion (Psalm 103:12). Confession reminds us that we are in a relationship with a God who loves us with *true love* exactly the way we are.

**Thanksgiving** (Psalm 92:1; Luke 19:11-19; Philippians 4:6; Colossians 3:15; 4:2; 1 Thessalonians 5:18). You will want to thank God for forgiving you of the sins that you confess, and you might then move on to thank God for many other things as well. Some people actually make lists of things for which they are thankful and take these into their prayer room as memory aids. You might list big-ticket items that we tend to take for granted (that I am alive, that I am healthy, that I live in a country where I am allowed to be free, that I have a job, that I have a house to live in, that I have a bed to sleep in at night), or smaller matters that we simply tend to overlook (that song on the radio, the taste of red wine, the feeling of my toes digging in wet sand, the sound of my cat's purr, the pleasure of a good night's sleep, the smell of burning wood). Of course, you need not limit your thanksgiving to good things that *you* experience. Once you begin thanking God for pleasures and blessings that come to *others,* your lists may become very long indeed. You will need notebooks, not index cards, to keep track of all the items for which you might (and sometimes *will*) give thanks. Do it. Filling those notebooks with lists of God's blessings (to you and to others) will be one of the most rewarding spiritual activities you will ever undertake.

**Supplication** (Jeremiah 33:3; Matthew 7:7; Philippians 4:6; Ephesians 6:18). We come last to supplication, which means "asking for stuff." Lots of people think that this is what prayer *is,* which is why I put it last. Of the four types of prayer discussed here, supplication is perhaps the least important, and we ought not jump to it immediately. We do well to remember the chronology of the Lord's Prayer: "*thy* name; *thy* kingdom; *thy* will" and then, "give *us*, forgive *us*, lead *us*, deliver *us*" (Matthew 6:9-13 RSV; italics mine). Simply put, the *thy, thy, thy* comes before the *us, us, us* (much less the *me, me, me*). Still, the Bible does encourage us to ask for what we want: "Ask, and it will be given you, search, and you will find; knock, and the door will be opened for you" (Matthew 7:7).

So, what should you ask for? Daily bread? World peace? The possibilities are endless, but, again, many people keep lists of things they want to pray for. I notice in my own church that when a child is baptized, the whole congregation

---

**SAMPLE PRAYERS THAT FOLLOW THE A-C-T-S PATTERN**

**A**—ADORATION
**C**—CONFESSION
**T**—THANKSGIVING
**S**—SUPPLICATION

**A** God, you are great,
**C** And we are small;
**T** We thank you for giving us this day,
**S** And ask that you help us to make the best of it.

**A** Jesus, I love you;
**C** I'm sorry I became annoyed with Peggy today.
**T** Thank you for forgiving me,
**S** And help me to be more patient with her tomorrow.

**A** God, you are powerful and merciful, a very present help in time of trouble.
**C** Something terrible has happened now and we are frightened;
**T** Thank you for being with us and understanding our fear.
**S** Give us your comfort. Give us your strength. Give us wisdom to know what to do next.

**A** Lord, I know that you are able to do anything,
**C** But I don't always know what to ask of you. I'm just going to tell you what I want,
**T** And I thank you for letting me do that.
**S** What I *want* to ask of you is . . .

---

is asked whether they will pray for this child to grow up in God's grace. Everyone responds, in unison, that they will. I sometimes wonder how many people actually do it. I know I would never remember if I didn't write it down. Prayer lists also serve to remind us when a prayer has been answered. One of my greatest pleasures in life is crossing things off lists, and it is a true spiritual delight to remember when something good happens that *I prayed for this*, and now I can cross it off the list (or move it to the "thanksgiving" folder). The box on pages 168–69 offers you a starter list, and if you are attentive to the world about you, you will be able to add many more items and categories of items to it. Or, if you're not a list-keeper, just be spontaneous—see what comes to mind as you reflect upon your own needs and the needs of others.

# Do We Get What We Pray For?

We have from Jesus an assurance that prayer will be heard. When Jesus himself prayed, he said, "Father, I thank you for having heard me. I knew that you always hear me" (John 11:41, 42). We have an assurance also that prayer will be answered: "Ask, and it will be given you" (Matthew 7:7). Of course, the "answer" can be a refusal (an old proverb holds that God can answer prayers by saying "Yes" or "No" or "Wait"), but if the answers were *always* refusals, the whole exercise of supplication would be a cruel joke. At least some of the time, we want to believe, God does things in response to our prayers. We want to think that prayer *makes a difference*.

The Bible gives many reasons why we might not get what we pray for: we ask out of selfishness (James 4:3); we have not repented of some sin (Isaiah 59:1-2); we have not forgiven someone (Mark 11:25); we pray with doubt or double-mindedness (James 1:5-7); we ask for things that are contrary to God's will (1 John 5:14). For that matter, the Bible indicates that husbands might find their prayers are hindered if they are not treating their wives properly, which in that day and age meant showing them the honor due "the weaker sex" (1 Peter 3:7). Some people make lists of reasons for unanswered prayer, and then, when they ask for something that doesn't happen, they go down the list, checking every item to try to determine the problem. Personally, I just don't think it works like that. There is a lot more mystery to prayer than could ever be taken into account by some trouble-shooting checklist. It's not some kind of a game with rules to help us win. The purpose of prayer is to bring us into a deeper relationship with God, not to persuade

God to give us things. The eventual goal of prayer should not be to bend God's will to our design: it should be to draw us closer to God until our will is bent to God's design. We begin by wanting God to give us what we desire, and we end by desiring what God wants to give.

Still, many people today find it hard to believe that *anything* will actually happen just because they pray for it. Such a notion seems to violate a modern understanding of the universe. Consider an example posed by Rabbi Harold Kushner: A high school senior holds an unopened letter from a college admissions office and prays, "Please, God, let it be an acceptance!" Will God alter the decision of the admissions office that has already been made and change the words of the letter in the envelope before it is opened? Rabbi Kushner says that God cannot do such things.[30] I disagree, partly because I think it is seldom a good idea to begin sentences with the words "God cannot . . ." (but see 2 Timothy 2:13). Still, I would say this: it may be *inappropriate* for God to do such a thing. God created the laws of nature that govern this universe of space and time, and it might not be right for God to disregard those laws for cavalier reasons (even if the reasons do not *seem* cavalier to our little minds). The Jewish Talmud (as Rabbi Kushner points out) lists things that one should *not* pray for: when a woman becomes pregnant, neither she nor her husband should pray for the child to be a boy (or a girl). The child's sex has already been determined, and God should not be expected to intervene after the fact.

I think that miracles, by definition, are rare, and that it is wrong for us to *expect* them, much less *demand* them. I do not quite agree with the Talmud that this means it is wrong to *ask*. On that point, I must go back to what I said in the beginning of this chapter: we come to God in prayer with the attitude of a child approaching a loving parent. We should feel comfortable telling God anything that we want and asking God to do whatever it is that we would like for God to do. Of course, we do not always realize the implications of our prayers. If I ask God to give me a good parking space, I am praying for someone else to have to walk farther than me. If I pray for my book manuscript to be accepted, I am asking for someone else's to be rejected (since most publishers only accept a set number of proposals each year). We live in a finite world where there are not enough good parking spaces or publishing contracts to go around. Why should God favor me over someone else? Why should I even ask God to do so? But the more we pray, the more we have to think about things like that. I do not pity the person who struggles with the question of how to pray right; I pity the person who never gives it a moment's thought. People who pray regularly end up having to think about things that

166

most people never think about, and, so, they travel avenues of spiritual growth and discovery known only to a few.

The bottom line for me is this: be honest in prayer. If someone says, "I really want a Corvette. Is it okay to ask God to give me one?" I am tempted to say, "Sure, go ahead, and see what happens." In that sense, prayer might be to spirituality what research is to science.[31] Prayer is an arena for encountering God and learning what kind of God we have. If we really do have the kind of God who hands out Corvettes to anyone who asks for them, I want to know that. If not, well, I want to know that too. So, pray for whatever you like, but as you *grow* in prayer, I think you will learn some things. The brother of our Lord writes, "You do not have because you do not ask," and then quickly adds, "You ask and do not receive, because you ask wrongly, in order to spend what you get on your pleasures" (James 4:3).

Some people say, "Be careful what you pray for." I say, "Well, yes, but don't be *too* careful." We need not worry that God will punish us for praying wrongly. Jesus once told his disciples, "If *you* . . . know how to give good gifts to your children, how much more will your Father in heaven give good things to those who ask him!" (Matthew 7:10; italics mine). If your child asks you for bread, would you give him a rock to eat instead? Or if she asks you for a fish, would you give her a snake? Of course not. But here's what I've learned about God: sometimes, we are just dumb enough to ask for rocks and snakes—and, then, God gives us bread and fish anyway.

Let me also say that I *do* believe prayer makes a difference. I believe that things do happen in this world that would not happen if someone did not pray. I'm not quite sure how it works, but I think the Bible teaches that this is the case (for example, James 5:14-18), and I think the experience of most people who pray often bears it out. I suspect that sometimes God does work miracles, and that even more often God finds ways of granting our requests without interrupting the normal flow of the universe. As the Anglican Archbishop William Temple is reported to have said, "It's amazing how many coincidences occur when one begins to pray." So I pray for the sick, and I believe that this helps in their healing. I pray for guidance and believe that my decisions are wiser than they would be if I didn't. I don't pretend to know how or why it works, but I believe it does. To quote Tennyson, "More things are wrought by prayer than this world dreams of" (*Idylls of the Kings*, "The Passing of Arthur").

Jesus prayed for God to remove the cup of suffering from him (Mark 14:36), and Paul asked God to relieve some affliction he called "a thorn in the flesh" (2 Corinthians 12:7-9). Neither request was granted, but the persons were not wrong to ask; both Jesus and Paul also believed that, in other instances, God did grant their requests. So, we need to know that God does not take orders from us, but we also need to know that the Bible encourages us to make all of our requests known to God (Philippians 4:6). We are little children stating our wishes and desires. Indeed, at times our prayers may be nothing more than expressions of "what we wish could be true," though we know at some level that it almost certainly cannot be. Such knowledge is *not* a lack of faith, and God (like any loving parent) wants to hear us speak of such things. We can pray seriously for that which we honestly believe God will grant, and we can pray wistfully for that which we merely fancy, and we can pray naïvely with little awareness of which of these is which. Sometimes God gives us what we want, sometimes God gives us nothing, and sometimes God surprises us with something much better.

I was in a grocery store one time where a mother was traversing the aisles with a young child seated in the cart. He kept pointing at everything they passed, whining, "I want *this*! Mommy, I want *this*!" It was a bit annoying, to be frank. Then, she took him out of the cart and held him and he was suddenly quiet. He didn't ask for anything more, and I thought, he didn't want *this* or *this*—he wanted her. Maybe he didn't know that was what he wanted, or how to ask for it, or even that it was an option. In any case, I think there is a parable here for one of the more important things we can learn about prayer and about God and about ourselves.

---

SUPPLICATION: A BEGINNING PRAYER LIST

One way to start a prayer list is by noticing what people pray for in the Bible and discovering what the Bible says that we should pray for. Here are a few suggestions, from Scripture, of things that you might consider putting on your prayer list:

- Pray for God to give you the Holy Spirit, not just once but repeatedly and constantly. Jesus said that the heavenly Father will give the Holy Spirit to all who ask (Luke 11:13).

- Pray for wisdom. James 1:5 says, "If any of you is lacking in wisdom, ask God, who gives to all generously and ungrudgingly, and it will be given you." Ask God to guide you in making important decisions in your life.

- Pray for strength to be the person God wants you to be. Martin Luther said, "Nothing is so necessary as to call upon God incessantly and drum into his ears our prayer that he may give, preserve, and increase in us all faith and obedience to the Ten Commandments." Bishop Phillips Brooks said, "Do not pray for easy lives—pray to be stronger persons! Do not pray for tasks equal to your powers but for powers equal to your tasks!" And Jesus said, "Watch and pray that you not enter into temptation; the spirit indeed is willing, but the flesh is weak" (Matthew 26:41 RSV).

- Pray for the Lord to "send out laborers into his harvest" (Matthew 9:38). Jesus told us to pray for this. I think what it means, for our day, is pray for God to call people into ministry, not just as pastors, but as people who serve God in all sorts of professions—school teachers, social workers, doctors, farmers, and so forth.

- Pray for the peace of Jerusalem (Psalm 122:6) and for peace in general.

- Pray for people who need God's help. This is called "intercessory prayer," and it is nothing more nor less than a simple act of love. Pray for your spouse, for your children, for your friends, for any couple that recently got married or divorced, for the sick and for the elderly and for the lonely and for the poor.

- Pray for your pastor. The apostle Paul repeatedly asked his parishioners to pray for him (see 2 Corinthians 1:11; Philippians 1:18-19; Ephesians 6:18-20; Colossians 4:3).

- Pray for governing authorities. The Bible says to do this (1 Timothy 2:1-2). I think it applies not only to political leaders, but also to your boss at work. From a strictly biblical perspective, people have no call to complain about their politicians or their boss if they aren't praying regularly for God to help and guide those leaders.

- Pray for your enemies. Again, Jesus *commanded* us to do this—not just to pray for our enemies to change, but to pray for God to bless them (Matthew 5:44; Luke 6:27-28). Try doing *that* regularly, and see what happens (to them and to you).

# CHAPTER EIGHTEEN

# A Strange Segue

There is a wonderful story in 2 Kings 5:1-14, about a military officer named Naaman, who contracts leprosy and travels across nations with horses and chariots and silver and gold to find the prophet Elisha, who might be able to heal him. When he arrives, Elisha is unimpressed by his retinue and simply counsels him to take a bath in the Jordan River. Naaman is infuriated and about to return home when his servants say, "If the prophet had commanded you to do something difficult, would you not have done it? How much more, when all he said to you was, 'Wash, and be clean'?" So the angry commander takes his bath, and, of course, he's healed.

Spirituality can be a bit like that. I notice people doing all sorts of things to become more spiritual—buying up crystals, sleeping in pyramids, taking pilgrimages, learning yoga. In the last few chapters of this book, I have suggested an Elisha-like approach: try going to church, reading the Bible, and saying your prayers. So many seem to think that this is way too simple. Perhaps it is—but if the path involved something more difficult, would you not try it?

# The Contemplative Life

In the seventeenth century, there was a monk named Brother Lawrence who determined that he would literally experience the presence of God at all times and in all places. By most accounts, he succeeded, such that those who knew him said there was no discernible difference between his demeanor when he was praying in chapel or scrubbing floors in the kitchen: he seemed equally in touch with God and with his own soul in either instance, having effectively dissolved any distinction between the mundane and the ethereal, between the secular and the sacred. Brother Lawrence left behind a book called *The Practice of the Presence of God,* which endeavors to train others to do what he did: develop an inward habit of mental orientation that is constantly focused on God. It is an art that he claims can be learned after weeks, months, and years of practice (with lapses and failures and returns).[32]

My goals are less lofty. I encourage you only (at this point) to develop some modest habits that might make your spiritual life more satisfying than it currently is. The practice of a private devotional time, which I have been touting for three chapters now, is a time-honored technique for exercising one's spiritual faculties and, at least, noticing the presence of God. In this chapter we will segue into a discussion of something else,

> I encourage you only (at this point) to develop some modest habits that might make your spiritual life more satisfying than it currently is.

but first I should indicate that, for centuries, personal devotions of spiritual pilgrims have often tended to follow a pattern referenced by four Latin terms: *lectio* (reading), *meditatio* (meditation), *oratio* (prayer), and *contemplatio* (contemplation, or "listening for God"). Traditionally, these four activities follow one another in a logical fashion that allows each element to flow out of its predecessor and build upon it. Thus, you might begin your devotions by reading a passage of Scripture. Then, close your eyes and sit quietly, meditating on what you have read. Don't puzzle over the meaning too much, but simply allow the words to sink in and note whatever feelings and impressions they make upon you. Then, respond to God in prayer, telling God what needs or desires were aroused within you as you meditated on this Scripture, or thanking God for blessings that came to mind as you did so. Then, sit silently and listen for God's response, for promptings of conscience or insight or imagination that you might boldly identify as the still, small voice of God.

The beautiful thing about such a pattern is that it is versatile enough for various applications. You could go through all four steps in a five-minute devotion on a single Bible verse, such as "Create in me a clean heart, O God" (Psalm 51:10) or "Blessed are the poor in spirit" (Matthew 5:3). But you could also use the pattern for a much longer devotion, in which you might read a larger amount of material or extend the amount of time reflecting upon it, praying to God, or listening for God's voice.

---

*Prayer catapults us on to the frontier of the spiritual life.*

Richard J. Foster

*Prayer enlarges the heart until it is capable of containing God's gift of himself.*

Mother Teresa

*Prayer is not to be undertaken with a mentality of success. The goal is neither to impress other people nor to impress God. The goal of prayer is simply to give oneself away.*

Emilie Griffin

*Prayer is something deeper than words. It is present in the soul before it has been formulated in words. And it abides in the soul after the last words have passed over the lips.*

Ole Hallesby

*To pray is to descend with the mind into the heart, and there to stand before the face of the Lord.*

Theophan the Recluse

*This was my method of prayer; as I could not make reflections with my own understanding, I contrived to picture Christ within me . . . my soul gained very much in this way because I began to practice prayer without knowing what it was.*

St. Teresa of Avila

*What then is the first rule of right prayer? Leave behind all thought of our own glory, cast aside all notion of our own worth, put away all self-assurance, humbly giving glory to the Lord.*

John Calvin

---

We have devoted a chapter apiece to Bible reading and to prayer. Now, I think we should consider the other two parts of this paradigm: meditation and contemplation. These are the quiet disciplines, more defined by *not-doing* than by *doing*. Hypothetically, then, they should be easy, but we all know how that goes. Inactivity does not come naturally to us. We smile at the irony: busy people who have to work at being inactive, who have to add "Spend Time Doing Nothing" to their "Things To Do" list. Smile, then, and realize how silly it is, how foolish we are. Then, do something about it. Do something about doing nothing.

**Meditation.** Many of the books on spirituality found in Christian bookstores emphasize that "Christian meditation" is different from the sort of meditation practiced in Eastern religions. The point, usually, is that Christian meditation consists of "filling the mind," while Eastern religions emphasize "emptying the mind." This is not quite true. First, Christianity *is* an Eastern religion (a Middle Eastern religion, to be exact). And second, while there are different varieties of meditation, Christians have always practiced *both* that which empties the mind and that which fills the mind—as have participants in most other religions. Having said this, however, I would agree with these books that the sort of meditation that "fills the mind" seems to be the most immediately accessible and advantageous variety for Western Christians to learn.

My first experience with meditation came when I was in high school. It was the sixties, and there was a certain fascination with gurus and the like. I joined a group of people who would sit in a circle and meditate. The leader told us the goal was to empty our minds completely and to think about nothing at all. I wasn't very good at this. Mostly, I just daydreamed and felt guilty for doing so. It was as if someone had told me, "Don't think about elephants," and the harder I tried *not* to think about elephants the more elephant-conscious I became. Of course, my adolescent and amateurish involvement with such rituals grants me no license to pass judgment on their value for sincere and practiced disciples. But, years later, I learned about this other form of meditation that seemed quite easy and was more quickly rewarding. It consists of sitting quietly and thinking deeply about God or faith or one's own spiritual needs. The emphasis is on *concentration,* on filling the mind with a particular thought or train of thought. It might take the form of what I described above, reflecting intently upon a passage of Scripture, but the process need not be limited to that. If you are at the seashore or out in a woods, you might meditate on the wonder of creation, noting colors and sounds and scents and thanking God for them. Paul gave the Philippians a perfect prescription for this sort of meditation when he said, "Whatever is true, whatever is honorable, whatever is just, whatever is pure, whatever is pleasing, whatever is commendable, if there is any excellence and if there is anything worthy of praise, think about these things" (Philippians 4:8).

"Be still, and know that I am God!" the Scripture says (Psalm 46:10). Sometimes, meditation is no more or less than that. Try just sitting, very quietly, with your eyes closed, and *know* that God is God. What pictures of God come into your mind? An old man with a beard? A ball of cosmic energy? A tender shepherd? A mighty warrior? Let the images roll through your mind, but not too quickly. Slow them down and reflect on each one, allowing it to develop with more detail. What if you were *seeing* God right now and later on would have to describe what you saw to a sketch artist? I know this is silly, but we are silly people and meditation allows us to get in touch with our silliness. It gives us a chance to recognize our images and conceptions of God, and it gives God a chance to enter our consciousness and alter or confirm those perceptions. What about the *attributes* of God? What qualities come to mind? Let them roll through your mind, but slow them down and think about each one. What does it mean to say that God is "slow to anger and abounding in steadfast love" (Nehemiah 9:17)? What does it mean to call God "righteous" (Psalm 119:137)?

If meditation on thoughts and sounds becomes rewarding (or even if it doesn't), you may eventually want to try something else. Try concentrating on the spaces between your thoughts, expanding them, slowing them down, or stretching them out. If you are in the woods or at the seashore, try concentrating on the silences between those sounds that would normally draw your attention. Do this, and you will come very close to discovering that *other* form of meditation, the one that consists of "emptying the mind." All sorts of thoughts will pop into your head; notice them, and let them pass on through. Think of those passing thoughts and feelings as passengers who are just along for the ride: don't try to get rid of them, but don't let them hijack your mind and take it somewhere else, either.

This is what some people call "centering prayer": allowing your spirit to come to a point of restful awareness that is not defined by any specific mental activity. The point is not to try as hard as you can to "think about nothing at all" (as I did when I was an adolescent), but to rest and allow the nothingness—the silences and the empty spaces in your thoughts—to evolve naturally in order to create a quiet, open space for noticing the presence of God. I am offering my own take on this sort of meditation now, and I should tell you that many teachers of Eastern religion (Christian and otherwise) would view the matter somewhat differently. But the cultural shift seems justified. We Westerners are so geared toward "filling the mind," rather than emptying it, that I say, go ahead and fill your mind—but fill it sometimes with nothingness. We tend to be much better at meditation that involves concentration than at that which involves detachment. So let's go with that—only concentrate sometimes on emptiness, focus sometimes on silence. And do not fear that you will turn into a Buddhist just by doing so.

**Contemplation**. The English word contemplation is pretty much a synonym for *meditation*, and wouldn't have to mean anything different. In devotional literature, however, the term *contemplation* is often used to refer to the spiritual practice of listening for God to speak to us. Ideally, prayer is conversation with God, not just a monologue. When we ask God for guidance, we should listen for an answer. We may obtain a sense of God leading us. We must be careful, of course, not to ascribe divine authority to our own thoughts, but we should be open to the possibility that God will speak to us through those thoughts.

I admit to having mixed feelings about this whole business of "hearing God speak to us." In the Bible, God sometimes talks out loud to people (1 Samuel 3:2-10) and, at other times, gives people very specific directions. God spoke to a man named Ananias and said, "Get up and go to the street called Straight, and at the house of Judas look for a man of Tarsus named Saul" (Acts 9:11). I don't know about you, but God never gives me street addresses or tells me with that kind of clarity exactly what I am to do. I don't hear voices like Joan of Arc did, either, unless you follow the interpretation given to that woman's story by George Bernard Shaw in his play *St. Joan.* In Shaw's version, the heroine is told that the voices she hears come from her own imagination, to which she replies, "I know, that is how God speaks to me." Similarly, I think that God can speak to me through my natural thought processes, and I think that prayerful contemplation enhances my ability to discern this voice of God amid the clutter of other voices in my head. On the one hand, I always want to be careful to distinguish between "Thus says the Lord" and "Thus thinks me." On the other hand, I don't want to drive too large a wedge between those concepts: God created my mind, and when I offer it to God prayerfully, God is able to use my mind to communicate with me.

We're not alone in this, and we should not trust in private revelations that remain untested by God's more certain public proclamations. God speaks to us through Scripture and through preaching and through the faithful testimonies of other people. Still, many Christians have found that when they contemplate matters prayerfully, listening for what God would say to them, their minds seem to work in ways that they might not have worked otherwise, in ways that ultimately seem more in keeping with what God would want. We know that God's ways are not our ways (Isaiah 55:8). But happy are those who delight in God's counsel, the Scripture says, and who contemplate God's ways day and night (Psalm 1:1-2).

# Mary and Martha

In the tenth chapter of Luke, Jesus pays a visit to the home of two sisters named Mary and Martha. The first sits at his feet and listens to his words. She has become a paradigm for the believer who practices what we have just been discussing, or, indeed, for any "spiritual person" who seeks intimacy with God. Her sister Martha is too busy for such pursuits and tells Jesus that Mary should be helping her with all the work that needs to be done. Jesus replies, "Martha, Martha, you are worried and distracted by many things; there is need of only one thing. Mary has chosen the better part, which will not be taken away from her" (Luke 10:41).

The point of the story is not to pit pietists against activists or to imply that one "personality type" is preferable to another. The point is simply *discerning the time*. There is a time to be busy and a time to be still. Mary knew what time it was; Martha did not. Luke wrote this story for people only a generation or so removed from the time of Jesus' ministry. His readers knew people who had known Jesus (compare Luke 1:2). How wonderful—they could only imagine—to have actually been there, to have met Jesus and heard him in person. Here is a story of two fortunate women who had that opportunity to spend an entire day with the Lord. Years later, an aged Mary would still be able to recall sitting at his feet, listening to his stories and insights. But when people asked her sister, "What was it like?" Martha would only be able to respond, "I don't know. I had a lot to do that day." How could anyone be too busy to spend time with Jesus when he was right there with them? In retrospect, what could have been *that* important?

The moral of the story is fairly obvious. I remember a retired chaplain telling me that he had heard over a thousand deathbed confessions. Such "last words" are confidential, he said, but he would allow this much: "I never heard anyone say, 'I wish I'd spent more time at the office.'" A chilling observation that we might all take to heart. But right now I want us to consider the lesson of the Mary and Martha story with reference to a matter that presses all those who seek closeness with God: the dichotomy (or is it continuity?) between private spirituality and service to society, between faith and works, between loving God and loving God's world.

There are those who wish to drive a wedge between the two. I was raised in a denomination that emphasizes social action and was warned from childhood against those who are "too heavenly minded to be any earthly good." I was told about people who pray about the world's problems all the time but don't actually get busy doing what needs to be done to make the world a better place. Now that I am (quite a bit) older, I have come to recognize that there is also a ditch on the other side of the road. Let us grant the existence of a "pious isolationist" trench, reserved for those who construe religion as "a private matter" and seek to develop some sort of highly individualized spirituality that in no way compels them to care for others. Personally, I think the number of persons who actually fall into such a trap has been exaggerated— most of the people I know who go to church on Sunday mornings or who read their Bibles or attend to private prayers every night do not do these things *instead* of volunteering at soup kitchens or campaigning for political candidates. In any case, I must direct your attention to the other side of the road, to a trench just teeming with persons who want to "live out their faith" by pursuing various worthwhile agendas while neglecting the nurture of their own souls.

We want to be of service to our world. We want to be useful, helpful, good people who make the world a better place. But, then, we must ultimately ask, "What do we have to offer?" I once heard Corrie ten Boom tell of an encounter she had with a frustrated minister, who said that he felt he "had given all for God" but still did not feel he had accomplished much in his ministry. Her humble observation: perhaps ministry depends not just on what we *give for God*, but also on what we *receive from God*. Likewise, I ask my seminary students how many of them are prepared to devote their lives to serving the Lord. Every hand goes up. Then I read them Mark 10:45 where Jesus says, "The Son of Man came not to be served but to serve." Jesus says he doesn't want you to serve him, I declare. He says that *he* wants to serve *you*. I'm messing with their minds, of course. There are plenty of Bible verses that do exhort us to serve the Lord (for example, Matthew 4:10 and 6:24), but seminarians are often more keen on serving than on being served. So are pastors. So are

177

*[handwritten margin notes: We cannot give that which we do not have — for God. To be seen in us we must have God with us — "Emmanuel" — Jesus Christ.]*

many of us. Peter would have gladly washed the feet of Jesus, but he didn't want to let Jesus wash *his* feet (John 13:6-8).

# The Mission of the Church

*The Mission of Jesus: to love the Church*

I offer the following proposition: *The mission of the church is to love Jesus Christ; everything else is just strategy.* If the church is "the bride of Christ," then the mission of the church first and foremost is to love the bridegroom. *How* we do that is an important question. Do we help the poor? Heal the sick? Keep the Ten Commandments? Strive for justice and peace in all the earth? Yes, we do all these things, and more besides, but we do them *as strategies,* as strategic initiatives that enact our love for Jesus.

"What do people who love Jesus do?" we asked in the second chapter of this book. They rejoice with an indescribable and glorious joy (1 Peter 1:8). They keep Christ's commandments (John 14:15, 21; 1 John 2:5; 5:3) and are attentive to his word (John 14:23, 24). They feed his sheep (John 21:15-17). They serve the saints (Hebrews 6:9) and love all of God's children (1 John 4:20—5:2).

Let's take just one of those references—the one that indicates people who love Jesus should "feed his sheep." Here is the full passage from John's Gospel:

> When they had finished breakfast, Jesus said to Simon Peter, "Simon son of John, do you love me more than these?" He said to him, "Yes, Lord; you know that I love you." Jesus said to him, "Feed my lambs." A second time he said to him, "Simon son of John, do you love me?" He said to him, "Yes, Lord; you know that I love you." Jesus said to him, "Tend my sheep." He said to him the third time, "Simon son of John, do you love me?" Peter felt hurt because he said to him the third time, "Do you love me?" And he said to him, "Lord, you know everything; you know that I love you." Jesus said to him, "Feed my sheep." (John 21:15-17)

Obviously, Jesus wants his sheep to be fed. It's an important matter, and figuring out exactly what it means to feed Jesus' sheep and how to do this in our modern world are significant subjects for our continued reflection. But let us also note that Jesus doesn't *just* want his sheep to be fed; he wants his sheep to be fed by someone who loves him. Attitude is often important in the Bible. God is not only concerned with behavior, but also with the heart—not only with *what* we do, but also with *why* we do it (see for example Matthew 6:1). Why does Jesus ask Peter three times "Do you love me?" For the church, mission is not just doing good things, but doing good things out of love for Jesus.

I admit to discomfort with language that seems to prioritize certain matters over others. Who am I to decide that one thing (loving Jesus) is primary and other things (everything else) secondary? Well, I would not want to decide that myself, but one time somebody did ask Jesus, "What is the greatest commandment of all?" He did not say, "Oh, there are lots of commandments, and they are all equally important." Nor did He say, the most important is "Feed my sheep" or "Help the poor" or "Include the marginalized" or whatever. He said, "The first and greatest commandment is this: Love the Lord your God with all your heart and soul and mind." That is the prime directive. Everything else flows from it, including the *second* commandment, "Love your neighbor as yourself" (see Mark 12:28-31).

> God is not only concerned with behavior, but also with the heart—not only with *what* we do, but also with *why* we do it.

One thing this means is that the *worship life of the church is an essential part of its mission.* We love our Bridegroom most purely and obviously when we worship, and whatever else we do should flow out of that worship as an extension of it. We exist as a church to worship God and to love Jesus, and one way that we worship God and love Jesus is by living the way that God wants us to live and doing the kinds of things that Jesus would have us do. It is common for some congregations today to identify worship with their church's "internal life" and mission (service to the world) with its "external life." One problem with such a construal is that worship should be external as well, for the focus of worship is properly on God, not on ourselves or on own needs. A more biblical model might describe the external mission of the church as being to love God (through worship) and to love neighbor (through service).

How did we get on this? Some may think it has been a strange segue. We began this chapter talking about private devotional practices and ended by trying to define the mission of the Christian church. I have done this deliberately, for the whole point is that the two are (or should be) continuous. The church can only offer the world what it receives from God, and individual believers can only be effective as servants *of* Jesus when they are served *by* Jesus. There is, or should be, something distinctive about good works performed by people of faith. If I am needy, I will accept help from any who offer it, but I would prefer to be helped by those who know that they are needy too. If I need advice, I will take it from anyone with insight, but I would prefer to heed the advice of one who is not too busy to sit sometimes and listen to the word of the Lord. And if I am a hungry sheep, I will accept food from any shepherd who can provide it, but I would prefer to be fed by a pastor who loves Jesus—and if she or he loves Jesus three times over, so much the better.

Avenues of love for Jesus

how we love Jesus is important. (Jn 21:15-17)

— philios — brotherly/family love.

— agape — Divine love.

① (Eros — sexual desire/love is not ment.)

"Simeon Peter — "do you agapé me?"

"...Lord, you know el philios you."

② — Feed my lambs

"Simeon, do you agape me?

Lord, you know el philos you.

— Feed my Sheep

③

Simeon, do you philios me?

Lord, you know everything —

'I love you.

— Feed my sheep.

# CHAPTER NINETEEN

# For the World

When Arthur Michael Ramsey was named Archbishop of Canterbury in 1961, he was asked by the media to describe his relationship with God. He said, "I enjoy Him." That answer was not what reporters had expected. Bishops, and surely *Arch*bishops, are often presumed to be staid and sophisticated clerics, not much given to enjoying anything. And God is often presumed to be austere and determined, benevolent perhaps, but not exactly enjoyable. The reporters need not have been surprised. About twenty years before the Archbishop's selection, one of his predecessors, William Temple, wrote in a statement of principles for the Anglican church that "Our value is our worth to God, and our end is to glorify God and enjoy Him forever." Similarly, The Shorter Catechism of the Presbyterian Church (dating from 1648) opens with the following exchange:

Q. What is the chief end of man (that is, humankind)?
A. Man's chief end is to glorify God and enjoy Him forever.

Most of us would probably like to have that kind of relationship with the Almighty: to be close to God in such a way that we actually *enjoy God* and take delight in God's presence. And so it should be, for such is the nature of love.

Every relationship of love has its rough spots, but couples in a healthy relationship experience joy, delight, and pleasure in each other's company. Of course, it is possible to love someone even if we do not like them very much, but we don't want our relationship with God to be like that. We don't want to love God the way we would love an enemy or an annoying neighbor, with a sort of begrudging love that we must summon up against our will. We want to love God with the sort of affection and devotion that comes easily and allows us to experience joy, delight, and pleasure in God's company.

*People who enjoy God seem to be people who enjoy life, and people who find delight and pleasure in God seem to be people who take delight and pleasure in the world that God has made.*

*Love the world w/ the love of God. JWC*

How can we love God like that? I'm sure I don't have all the answers, but I think that reaching such a level of spirituality has something to do with our relationship with the world in which we live, and with our evaluation of life itself. I do *not* mean this in the sense that some people would think—withdrawal from the world or renunciation of life's pleasures. Quite the contrary. People who enjoy God seem to be people who enjoy *life*, and people who find delight and pleasure in God seem to be people who take delight and pleasure in the world that God has made.

When I was a child, the pastor of our church used to read us stories by Barbara Jurgensen, a spiritual author of the time who fashioned fanciful parables for the modern world. This was one of his favorites:

Petronius stood with his weight on one foot, then on the other. The line ahead of him was moving so slowly that it would be ages before he got his turn at the Judgment Seat.

Then he picked up his nose. What was that delicious smell?

He leaned out of line and saw an angel coming along the line carrying a tray of hot-buttered rolls, holding out the tray to each person.

Petronius had been standing in line so long that he was very hungry. And in a few minutes the angel would be offering him a—

Then he suddenly realized—he must *not* take a roll. All his life he had done his best to avoid being carried away by pleasure. He had seen too many people live only for their own enjoyment and had made up his mind that he would not be one of them. For years, therefore, he had deliberately ignored pleasurable things in order to concentrate his attention more fully on serving God.

The story continues, as Petronius awaits his judgment. He must pass by a bed of fragrant red flowers, and then a cute little kitten beckons him to pet it. He surmises that he is being "tested," to determine if he can keep his focus on godly things amid these varied distractions. Then (predictably for adults, but not for children), we reach the ironic conclusion:

> Petronius heard God saying, "Well done, my son, I'm glad you have come home. There's just one thing. . . ." Then Petronius noticed that God had something on his lap—a small yellow and white kitten. On the table next to God's throne he noticed a vase of the fragrant flowers he had forced himself to ignore. And a plate with a half-eaten roll.

The moral of the story, according to Jurgensen, is that people will have to give an account to God on the day of judgment for all the good things they failed to enjoy.[33]

I learned this story as a child, but I soon forgot it as an adult. I fell quickly into the trap that snares many Christians, believing that "worldly" is the opposite of "spiritual" and that people who want to be spiritual have to work hard at not being worldly. Theologians know that this is a very old misconception, or indeed "heresy" as they like to call it. Quite early in the history of the Christian church, a movement called *Gnosticism* arose that pitted all that was spiritual against all that was material, fleshly, or worldly. Many Christians were attracted to this movement, and, for a few centuries, there were Christian Gnostics (as well as other types of Gnostics). In its most extreme form, Gnosticism taught that the God of the Old Testament was an evil demon who had created the material world as a prison for what were once free and independent souls, and who had likewise created physical human bodies as individual prisons for individual souls. Only by renouncing all that was fleshly and material could the trapped souls get free and go back to whatever they had been doing (floating around the cosmos?) before they got caught and put in bad human bodies in a bad earthly world.

Obviously, most Christian (and Jewish) leaders opposed these ideas and denounced them, and, eventually, the religion of Gnosticism (in any official sense) became extinct. But the *ideas* did not go completely away, and, in less extreme forms, they have persisted to this day: souls are good, bodies are bad (or, at least, not as good as souls); the purpose of religion is to feed the soul and free it from the confines of a material world. These lingering, quasi-gnostic ideas have continued to affect Christian attitudes toward all sorts of things, including spirituality.

I never became a Gnostic, but I did fall into thinking that the best way to enhance my spiritual proclivities was to disengage from the world as much as possible. Most of the Christians I knew seemed to think (or just assume) that this was how it worked. I was also reading the Bible quite a bit, and I found exhortations there that seemed to support this way of thinking. We should store up treasure in heaven (Matthew 6:20) and set our minds "on things that are above, not on things that are on earth" (Colossians 3:2). Nevertheless, I constantly ran into one very big problem: Jesus.

## The Human God

The mere *fact* of Jesus was perplexing. Christians believe that, in the person of Jesus, God came to us as a human being. God took on human flesh and lived a fully human life. Indeed, the God whom Jesus reveals to us is a God who thoroughly enjoys being human. The biblical story of Jesus is that of a remarkably physical and sensual person. In fact, Jesus stands out from his contemporaries in just this regard, as someone who appreciates life's pleasures and participates gladly in what the world has to offer.

He may be contrasted, first of all, with the Pharisees. Throughout the Gospel stories, these stereotyped opponents of Jesus are presented as paragons of a world-renouncing faith that is strikingly different from Jesus' own world-affirming stance. For example, the Pharisees are very strict in their observance of Sabbath regulations and religious dietary restrictions, while Jesus seems a bit cavalier, proclaiming broadly that people should feel free to do whatever is "good" on the Sabbath (Matthew 12:12) and claiming that no one can be defiled spiritually by what they eat (Matthew 15:11). The Pharisees are also careful about the company they keep, while Jesus, to their chagrin, freely associates with "tax collectors and sinners" (Luke 15:1-2). Further, the Pharisees are strongly committed to fasting and seem to be especially adept at it (Luke 18:12), while Jesus loves banquets and encourages feasting. Bible scholars often observe with a smile that, in the Gospel of Luke, Jesus appears to be "always eating"—at any given point, he seems either to be at a meal, on his way to a meal, or coming from a meal. He also talks about meals a lot. When he needs an image for the kingdom of heaven, he chooses that of a big party at which "a fatted calf" will be consumed, and at which there will be loud music and dancing (Luke 15:23-25).

We need not go overboard with these observations. First, it needs to be said (repeatedly) that the Pharisees portrayed in our Gospel stories were in no way typical of Jewish people in the first century, nor are they typical of Jewish people today—their foibles are meant to illustrate human traits, not Jewish ones. Further, Sabbath observance, kosher rules, and fasting can be meaningful spiritual disciplines, and one can show discretion with regard to personal associations without yielding to elitism or bigotry. The point we want to take away from these stories is simply that Jesus—our prime representative of God—was notoriously lax with regard to such matters. He did not fulfill the expectations that most people would have had for what a religious or spiritual person should be like. It wasn't that he didn't pray or cite the Scriptures or talk about God in his daily life—he did do all those things, but with regard to the Sabbath and his friendships and his general lifestyle, he was just, well, *worldly!*

And then there was John the Baptist. Jesus would seem to have had more in common with him than with anybody else, but there was one huge difference. John was what theologians would call an "ascetic," and Jesus was anything but that. While Jesus feasted at those numerous banquets, John lived out in the desert and ate whatever he could find (locusts and honey). John also refrained from drinking wine, while Jesus earned a reputation as a conspicuous wine-drinker (Luke 7:34). People noticed these things and thought that John and Jesus were very different prophets. John was like someone playing a dirge and expecting his audience to mourn. Jesus was like someone playing the flute and expecting his audience to dance (Luke 7:31-34).

As the story unfolds, we see just how different these two prophets are. John is primarily concerned with getting people to repent of their sins (Matthew 3:2), and he does not shirk even from confronting the most powerful of political rulers with their transgressions (Mark 6:18). In this manner he is heroic, and with regard to opposition to sin he and Jesus are very much alike. But Jesus does more than proclaim repentance and threaten people with God's judgment. He is also, for instance, concerned with healing the sick, restoring people to a place where they can enjoy life in all its fullness. John the Baptist was a great man of God, but it is frankly hard to imagine him spending an afternoon chatting to a Samaritan woman beside a well (John 4:7-42) or holding children on his lap and telling them stories (Mark 10:16). It is *really* hard to imagine him becoming concerned that a couple's wedding reception might be ruined by a shortage of liquor (John 2:1-11). Nowhere does John ever claim that he wants everyone in this world to experience life *abundantly* (compare John 10:10). Indeed, there is no hint anywhere in the biblical material that this great man of God ever enjoyed his own life. There is no hint that he liked being alive in this world or, for that matter, that he even liked *people* very much.

Again, let us not go overboard. Jesus has nothing but praise for John (Luke 7:24-28). He does not disparage John's path, but it is not his own. And our model for spirituality is Jesus, who seemed to like all sorts of people, including not only children and Samaritans and wedding guests who drink too much, but also lepers and tax collectors and centurions and all sorts of folk whom prophets and rabbis would not usually count among their associates. We should mention that he also appears to have enjoyed the company of women, allowing (or even inviting) them to be among his closest companions as he traveled about the countryside in a manner that some must have thought controversial (Luke 8:1-3). On two different occasions, we hear of women anointing Jesus with oil, rubbing the cologne into his skin with their hands and hair (Luke 7:36-50; Mark 14:3-9). He gets criticized both times that this happens. Once, a Pharisee is appalled because the woman performing the action is apparently a person of questionable character or "ill repute." The other time, his own disciples consider the anointing to be a frivolous excess and complain that the money wasted on his perfume could have been better spent on something else. There is a remarkable pattern in these Gospel stories: Jesus is regularly criticized by friends and foes alike for *not being spiritual enough*, for being too indulgent, too sensual, and too materialistic.

Most people in Jesus' day would have looked at Jesus and thought that he was a very worldly person. In fact, they *did* think this. They saw the Pharisees and they saw John the Baptist and then they looked at Jesus and said, "Look, a glutton and a drunkard, a friend of tax collectors and sinners" (Luke 7:34). Basically, then, they had two complaints: (1) he likes *worldly things* too much, and (2) he likes *worldly people* too much. His fondness for the first (food and drink) makes him "a glutton and a drunkard"; his fondness for the second makes him "a friend of tax collectors and sinners."

So, let's return to my adolescent quest for spirituality and "the problem of Jesus." Jesus was the most spiritual person who ever lived—the very embodiment of God. But Jesus apparently liked parties with loud music and dancing—he thought that was an image of heaven. He loved to eat and thought the perfect banquet meal was fatty red meat (veal, to be specific). He liked drinking wine and, when facing death, stated his one regret as being that he would not be able to drink it again until reunited with his disciples in the consummation of the kingdom (Matthew 26:29). He appreciated having women massage his feet, and he allowed himself the occasional luxury of expensive ointment (when it was a gift).

*Jesus is regularly criticized by friends and foes alike for not being spiritual enough, for being too indulgent, too sensual, and too materialistic.*

And so the question: if true spirituality—being close to God—is achieved by renouncing worldly pleasures and attaining a higher plane than vulgar human existence, then why did God become a human being, and—more to the point—why did God become *this* human being? What was God trying to tell us by entering "vulgar human existence" and then enjoying it so thoroughly? I wondered about this, and then I remembered the Barbara Jurgensen story I had been told as a child.

Here, then, is another point for what I call the second naïveté (page 12): spirituality is not to be achieved by negating the world or by renouncing what life has to offer us; rather, true spirituality is experienced through recognizing the world as God's world and embracing all that life has to offer us. People who love Jesus must allow no divide between "spirituality" and "worldliness." In Jesus, all that is spiritual takes on earthly flesh and *becomes worldly.* For people who love Jesus, then, the quest for spirituality is also a quest for earthiness and humanity. The more we love God, the more we will love God's world; the more we enjoy God, the more we will enjoy God's world and revel in its pleasures.

## Love the World

The basic principle is this: *we love the world that Jesus loved.* God created the world and declared it good (Genesis 1:31). The fall from Paradise did nothing to change this basic goodness, for even after centuries of human sin, a psalmist could declare, "The earth is (still) the Lord's and all that is in it!" (Psalm 24:1).

Why, then, does the Bible also say, "Do not love the world or the things in the world" (1 John 2:15)? Biblical scholars tell us that such texts were born out of abject persecution when Christians lived in a world that was overtly hostile and intent on destroying their faith. As such, we are told, such texts might not apply to modern Western Christians who for the most part live in happier times. I actually think there's more to it than that. The exhortation relates to conversion: people who come to faith must renounce the world of unbelief and the culture of sin from which they have been set free. They must not live in *that* world, which would enslave them or entice them away from faith in God. Still, the injunction should never be construed as meaning, "Do not love God's creation or the pleasures it provides."

So what does it mean to "love the world that Jesus loved"? People often say it means that we should be "in the world but not of it." That sounds right, but I'm not quite sure what it means. Prepositions are the trickiest words in the English language and, when people say "*in* the world but not *of* it," I'm never exactly sure what they mean by *in* and what they mean by *of*. Still, I think I can come up with four corollaries to my basic principle: love the world that Jesus loved.

1. ***Enjoy* the world as Jesus enjoyed it.** We've talked about this enough already. Smell the flowers, pet the kitten, eat the roll. Julian of Norwich said, "The greatest honor we can give to God is to live gladly because of his love."

2. ***Live* in the world as Jesus lived in it.** Luke's two-volume work (the Gospel and Acts) seems to portray Jesus and the church in a pattern modeled on that of Elijah and Elisha. The latter is the Bible's clearest example of a sequel prophet, known primarily for doing and saying the same things as his mentor. Elisha is less famous than Elijah because, even though he did some amazing things, they had all been done before. The Gospel of Luke and the book of Acts seize upon this imagery: after Jesus ascends into heaven (as Elijah did—see 2 Kings 2:1-12), his mantle of power (the Holy Spirit) falls upon his followers, who then begin to duplicate in Acts the things that Jesus himself had done in the Gospel. Peter and Paul even heal the sick and raise the dead, but, notably, they are not proclaimed to be messiahs or saviors, and no one starts religions or founds churches to worship them. No follower of Jesus can ever take the place of Jesus, but Christians can and should continue to live as Jesus lived and to do what he did. No greater compliment attends the work of Christians than this: "It's been done before."

Many theologians made fun of the "What Would Jesus Do?" bracelets that became popular a few years back. Obviously, making ethical decisions in our modern world gets a lot more complicated than such a simple question implies. How would a first-century peasant respond to modern technology and the problems it poses? Still, the bracelet craze was not a bad thing, as fads go. Is there really anything wrong with millions of Americans (mostly teenagers) asking themselves such a question and evaluating their conduct and lifestyle in just such a light? Luther said that we are all to be "little Christs" in this world. And about a century before Luther, Thomas à Kempis wrote his spiritual classic, *Imitation of Christ*, a work that continues to be respected even by those who snickered at the WWJD bracelets. Though the issues we face may differ, we can come to know the values that guided Jesus throughout his life and ministry and then try to apply those values to our own decision making. This, for instance, is what puts the brakes on our otherwise insatiable drive for amusement and prevents our enjoyment of earthly pleasures from becoming irresponsible hedonism. Some pleasures may be harmful to us or to others; some may be disrespectful or simply disgraceful in ways that our limited perspective would not recognize, which is why we must trust in the instruction of Scripture and in the counsel of our spiritual advisors and faith communities. Jesus calls us to self-denial (Mark 8:34) and reminds us that even when our spirit is willing our flesh can be weak (Mark 14:38). The apostle Paul is a bit more blunt in asserting that the desires of God's Spirit and of our flesh are opposed to each other, so that we (often) should *not* do what we would like to do (Galatians 5:17). Everyone who's lived very long or, at least, very perceptively, knows that this is true.

*Joy in life, make a long life*

3. **Care for the world as Jesus cared for it.** In the beginning, God *enjoyable* appointed Adam (and eventually Eve) to care for the earth (Genesis 2:15). *JWC* That charge remains with us today and is all the more important now that human beings possess unprecedented capacities for destruction. Jesus did not have much opportunity to express concern for what we would call *ecology*, but he did seem dedicated to restoring the world to the healthy condition that God intended. This is most evident in his miracles of healing: people are not supposed to be blind or deaf or leprous or paralyzed. By extension, we might surmise that lakes are not supposed to be polluted, forests are not to be wantonly destroyed, the ozone layer is not to be dissipated, and so forth. Jesus fixed what he could, and we must do the same.

4. **Suffer for the world as Jesus suffered for it.** Jesus died for us and for the world, and all who are baptized into him come to share in that

*One will, or can only suffer in a place in which they exist. (JWC)*
*Joy also comes to us in the world, because joy is known to those who have life.*

death (Romans 6:3). As Dietrich Bonhoeffer put it, "When Jesus Christ calls someone, he bids them come and die."[34] Talk of suffering and death is not pleasant, but if we love Jesus, and if we love the world that Jesus loved, then we must be willing to suffer for the sake of this world, even as Jesus suffered for it. This might mean, first, that we must sometimes suffer for our own sake. When we are baptized, we invite God to put to death anything within us that prevents our life in this world from being what God would want it to be. That is a lifelong process, and, so, when things are going as they should, the baptized will feel like they are dying a little bit every day. Beyond this, however, we may also suffer for others, for we relate to Jesus and to God as part of a community, and we should be willing to bear the burdens of others (Galatians 6:2). Indeed, when we are secure in our love for Jesus, we will suffer even for those we do not know, for the oppressed or the helpless, or for future generations yet to be born. We suffer *for the world* for no other reason than that we have come to love Jesus, and, since he loves this world, we too will love the world that he loves.

"the baptized will believe that they are made alive in Christ - eternally. JWC.

Christ's suffering saves us, for in Jesus' suffering we see that, even if we suffer, the end result is Redemptive not necessarily Retribution. JWC

# CHAPTER TWENTY

# The Great Truth

We have probably all seen bumper stickers that say, "Smile! God loves you!" It is a happy announcement, though we might not always appreciate being advised or even commanded to respond to it in the manner that some anonymous motorist has deemed appropriate. It is actually more than just a happy announcement. The three words, "God loves you," express the most profound truth in the universe. They express a dictum that ultimately escapes the deepest of philosophical inquiries and that carries implications beyond anything that savants or sages, much less evangelistic motorists, have been able to fully apprehend or appreciate.

Moses told the redeemed Israelites that "it was because the Lord loved you" that God delivered them from centuries of bondage in Egypt (Deuteronomy 7:7-8). Later, this same God would be moved to rescue the people again for one simple reason: "Because you are precious in my sight, and honored, and I love you" (Isaiah 43:4). In the New Testament, we hear that "God so loved the world that he gave his only Son" (John 3:16). Later, when facing his darkest hour, this Son prays for one thing above all else: "that the world may know that you have sent me and have loved them" (John 17:23). Apostles speak often of the God "who has loved us" (2 Thessalonians 2:16; see also Romans 5:8; Ephesians 2:4; 1 John 3:1; 4:9; 4:16). Paul declares that nothing "can separate us from the love of God" (Romans 8:35, 39) and testifies that "the life I now live in the flesh I live by faith in the Son of God, who loved me and gave himself for me" (Galatians 2:20).

All cynicism, apprehension, suspicion, and fear, all hostility and dread, all of our bitterness and belligerence, our malevolence and misanthropy, run up against this one great truth that transcends time and space. This truth is easily dismissed by those who cherish their dysfunctions, unable or unwilling to imagine how they would get along without them. It is derided as simplistic, discarded as wishful thinking, lampooned, scorned, and denied for any reason and with every excuse. The mortal mind works overtime to construct defenses against the implications of what, in the depths of our souls, we nonetheless all sense to be true.

This is what is true:

- We are loved by God.
- We are loved by the universe, for God is its creator.
- We are loved by life, for God is its source.
- We are loved by love itself, for God *is* love.

When you love the world about you—your part of the universe—you are only responding to its love for you. If you are, or someday become, one of those wonderful people who loves life, you will only be responding to life's love for you. And should you be, or become, one of the truly fortunate ones who loves *love*, you will know already without being told that you are only responding to that which has sought you and found you and truly loved you first.

I don't care if this sounds trippy or New-Agey or whatever. The medium may be the message, as Marshall McLuhan said, but truth withstands ignominies of packaging. The love of God is a truth revealed to infants (Matthew 11:25) and praised by sucklings (Matthew 21:16). Small wonder, then, that it is not often described in terms adequate to its gravity. What would such terms be? Who will measure the depth and breadth of such a love? Who will explain a love that is *by definition* beyond knowing (Ephesians 3:19)? But whether emanating from the lips of a tortured martyr or plastered above the exhaust pipe of an old gray Ford, the simplest affirmation of God's love judges and trivializes all other attempts at making sense of our complicated existence. Knowing God and growing close to God begins and ends with this truth.

And now I will tell you a mystery, something that I am only beginning to realize. I think perhaps this will be the *next* point for the charting of my growth in naïveté (page 12), but my appreciation for *this* point is yet too embryonic to qualify as something I have learned. It is something I hope to learn, if (contrary to my personal expectations) our Lord should tarry.

The question is, simply, *Why* does God love us? Christian teachers often say that God loves us solely because God is so loving and not in the least because we are lovable. We must never think that there is anything in us to attract God's love. We are miserable and despicable sinners, yet God takes mercy on us and loves us *in spite of what we are*. This is a testimony to grace, the pinnacle and hallmark of Christian doctrine. But in articulating the matter thus, I think that Christians sometimes fail to discern the true mystery of God's love. The problem is not that they have overemphasized grace but, indeed, that they have underestimated grace, reducing it to pity. Perhaps the teaching that "God loves us in spite of

> Whether emanating from the lips of a tortured martyr or plastered above the exhaust pipe of an old gray Ford, the simplest affirmation of God's love judges and trivializes all other attempts at making sense of our complicated existence. Knowing God and growing close to God begins and ends with this truth.

what we are" is not so much *wrong* as it is naïve. It is a simple expression of a first naïveté that attaches grace to redemption rather than creation. Luther, as usual, gets it right: "we are not loved because we are lovely, but we are lovely because we are loved" (*Heidelberg Disputation*, 28). We are lovely and we are lovable because God, in love, has made us to be lovely and lovable.

When Jesus was born in Bethlehem, angels sang to shepherds and offered this doxology:

> Glory to God in the highest
> And on earth:
> Peace among men [that is, people]
> With whom God is pleased.

Many Bible readers have taken this verse (Luke 2:14, quoted here from the RSV) to mean that God bestows peace upon those people who please God, but not upon others. The translators of the NRSV appear to have taken it this way: "On earth peace among those whom he favors!" This is almost certainly wrong, for the full context of Luke's story reveals an extraordinarily generous God who proffers salvation to all humanity, and even to all *flesh* (Luke 3:6)—this, incidentally, is my proof text for arguing that our pets may be with us in heaven, and, personally, I do expect three of my four cats to make it there; I refrain from speculation regarding the destiny of the fourth). The meaning of the angel's proclamation is that God wishes for there to be peace on earth among human beings. Why? Because human beings—people, the human species—are intrinsically pleasing to God. God favors not just "some humans" but *humanity*. God is pleased with "people" and blesses "people" with peace.

A similar thought is expressed in another oddly ignored and often mangled text. The brief epistle to Titus makes a passing reference to the *philanthrōpia* of God our Savior (Titus 3:4). The meaning of that word may be evident even to those who haven't studied Greek. The first part, *phil,* means *love* (as in "philosophy," the love of wisdom, or Philadelphia, the city of brotherly love); the second part, *anthrōpia,* means humanity (as in "anthropology," the study of humans). The Scripture is saying, in no uncertain terms that God our Savior loves humans or, indeed, humanity or, simply, humanness. Still, Bible translators are apt to water this down, referring to God's "loving kindness" (both RSV and NRSV), rather than to God's "love for humanity." Why they would do so is anybody's guess, but I suspect an intrusion of the first naïveté: it is easier to believe that God is loving and kind than to believe that God loves *humans* or *humanity* or *humanness* itself. But, of course, that is what the Bible teaches. Humans—humanity—humanness . . . it was all God's idea in the first place.

> The Scripture is saying in no uncertain terms that God our Savior loves humans or, indeed, humanity or, simply, humanness.

The biblical truth is this: God loves us, not in spite of what we are but because of what we are, because we are *essentially* and *ultimately* the lovely and lovable people whom God in grace made us to be. We may become miserable and despicable in our sins, but that does not and cannot cancel out the fact that we were created in the image of God (Genesis 1:26). And, then, through Jesus Christ, God works a new creation (2 Corinthians 5:17): our sins are washed away and God sees us for what we are, people destined to be holy and blameless (Ephesians 1:4).

The Bible, we have observed, often uses the metaphor of a married couple to describe our relationship with God, and, because the Bible was written in an era even more patriarchal than our own, God is consistently portrayed as the groom in such encounters and we, as the bride. In the New Testament, the image becomes Christ and the church, but even before that, in what we now call the Old Testament, there was God and Israel. When that nation was naughty, a prophet like Hosea could insist that God had married her out of pity, taking a harlot for a wife and bestowing upon her honor she did not deserve. Such texts continue to feed the guilt-driven homilies of some preachers, and there is partial truth in the imagery that we must not avoid. But happier prophets tell the story differently. See, now, Isaiah 62:1-5. "You shall be called by a new name," God promises, invoking the ancient tradition of a bride taking her husband's name in marriage. And what will God's bride be called? It will be a name that "the mouth of the Lord will give." All right, so what will it be? The prophet builds suspense in this way for a few verses, and of course we assume the name will be "Beloved by God" or something like that—something that testifies to the greatness of God's love. No. Here it is: "You shall be called 'My Delight is in Her.'" A bit cumbersome, but very much to the point. And why shall we be called this? Because "the Lord delights in you." And then the grand conclusion: "As the bridegroom rejoices over the bride, so shall your God rejoice over you." *Beulah* —

A faithful spouse is a good thing. An adoring spouse may be even better. We should be content, perhaps, if God were likened only to the first, but Isaiah likens God to the second as well. What greater thrill can come to those who are in love than to have their beloved be proud of them, take delight in them, rejoice over them? "You shall be a crown of beauty," God says (Isaiah 62:3). God not only loves us, but *adores* us. God thinks we are beautiful and is proud to have us. God loves us, not in spite of what we are, but because of what we are, although a part of what we *are* is what we *shall be* when the work of God is complete in us. *God's finished work — God's Sabbath Rest*

Grace is more than pity. God *made us* to be lovable, and so we are. God's love is not blind or silly, but based on perception clear and profound. Indeed, God sees things in us that we might not see in ourselves, including our potential, or even better, our destiny. God adores us not out of foolish infatuation, but because we are, in fact, adorable. God takes delight in us not because God is easily delighted, but because we are indeed delightful. God loves us not because God is too dense or generous to see us as we are, but because we actually are essentially and ultimately lovely.

This is the great truth that cuts into our complicated lives. Loving Jesus begins and ends with this truth. Loving Jesus is our way of coming closer to

*Comes to us in Christ. We enter into Sabbath into our Relationship in which we Rest in the presence of the One who loves us best of all*

this God, of adoring the God who adores us, of taking delight in the God who delights in us, of loving the God who loves us first.

---

**EVERLASTING LOVE**

- God says to Israel, "I have loved you with an everlasting love" (Jeremiah 31:3).

- "Having loved his own who were in the world, he [Jesus] loved them to the end" (John 13:1).

- "Who will separate us from the love of Christ? Will hardship, or distress, or persecution, or famine, or nakedness, or peril, or sword? . . . No, . . . I am convinced that neither death, nor life, nor angels, nor rulers, nor things present, nor things to come, nor powers, nor height, nor depth, nor anything else in all creation, will be able to separate us from the love of God in Christ Jesus our Lord" (Romans 8:35-39).

- "So we have known and believe the love that God has for us. God is love, and those who abide in love abide in God, and God abides in them" (1 John 4:16).

- "Keep yourselves in the love of God" (Jude 21).

---

1. Richard J. Foster, *Prayer: Finding the Heart's True Home* (San Francisco: HarperSanFrancisco, 1992), 3.

2. In this book, I sometimes use the phrases "loving God" and "loving Jesus" in ways that are virtually synonymous. I do this, I hope, with full appreciation of trinitarian doctrine. By *God,* I mean "the God made known to us in Jesus Christ" and by *Jesus,* I mean "the Son of God, through whom God is made known."

3. I owe this entire section to Erick Nelson, a pious theologian who does as fine a job of integrating heart and mind as anyone I've ever known.

4. C. S. Lewis, *Mere Christianity* (New York: Macmillan, 1960), 120.

5. Eugene H. Peterson, "Missing Ingredient: Why Spirituality Needs Jesus," *Christian Century,* March 22, 2003, 30.

6. Marcus J. Borg, *Meeting Jesus Again for the First Time: The Historical Jesus and the Heart of Contemporary Faith* (San Francisco: HarperSanFrancisco, 1994), 15.

7. Peter Gilquist, *Let's Quit Fighting about the Holy Spirit* (Grand Rapids, Mich.: Zondervan, 1974), 108.

8. Lewis, *Mere Christianity,* 145.

9. C. S. Lewis, *The Great Divorce* (New York: Macmillan, 1946), 23–29.

10. C. S. Lewis, *A Grief Observed* (New York: Seabury Press, 1961), 36.

11. Evelyn Underhill, *Worship* (New York: Harper, 1936).

12. C. S. Lewis, *The Four Loves* (London: Geoffrey Bles), 48.

13. C. S. Lewis, "Answers to Questions on Christianity (1944)," in *God in the Dock: Essays on Theology and Ethics,* ed. Walter Hooper (Grand Rapids, Mich.: Eerdmans, 1970), 61–62.

14. Letter of Viet Dietrich to Philip Melancthon, contained now in St. Louis edition of *Luthers Werke,* vol. 16, 1763.

15. John Wesley, cited in Tony Castle, *The New Book of Christian Quotations* (New York: Crossroad, 1984), 192.

16. John Bunyan, cited in Harry Emerson Fosdick, *The Meaning of Prayer* (New York: Young Men's Christian Association, 1915), 81.

17. Henri J. M. Nouwen, *The Only Necessary Thing: Living a Prayerful Life* (New York: Crossroad, 1999), 91.

18. Thomas Merton, *New Seeds of Contemplation* (Norfolk, Conn.: New Directions, 1962), 82–83.

19. Thomas Watson, "How We May Read the Scriptures with Most Spiritual Profit," in *Puritan Sermons,* vol. 2 (Wheaton, Ill.: Richard Owen Roberts, 1981), 62.

20. Dietrich Bonhoeffer, *The Way to Freedom* (New York: Harper & Row, 1966), 59.

21. Anthony Bloom, *School of Prayer* (London: Darton, Longman, and Todd, 1970), 58–59.

22. Thomas Merton, cited in Ann Monroe, *The Word* (Louisville, Ky.: Westminster John Knox, 2000), 209.

23. Geoffrey Thomas, *Reading the Bible* (Edinburgh, Scotland: The Banner of Truth Trust, 1980), 22.

24. Richard Foster, *Celebration of Discipline: The Path to Spiritual Growth* (San Francisco: HarperSanFrancisco, 1978), 31.

25. Evelyn Underhill, *Concerning the Inner Life* (New York: E. P. Dutton & Co., 1926), 14, 18.

26. Henri J. M. Nouwen, *With Open Hands*, rev. ed. (Notre Dame, Ind.: Ave Maria Press, 1995), 84.

27. Ole Hallesby, *Prayer* (Minneapolis: Augsburg Publishing House, 1931), 25.

28. Nouwen, *With Open Hands*, 80.

29. C. S. Lewis, *The Problem of Pain* (New York: Macmillan, 1962), 58–59.

30. Harold S. Kushner, *When Bad Things Happen to Good People* (New York: Avon Books, 1981), 116.

31. P. T. Forsythe, cited in Thomas Merton, *Contemplative Prayer* (Garden City, N.J.: Doubleday, 1969), 11.

32. Brother Lawrence, *The Practice of the Presence of God with Spiritual Maxims* (Old Tappen, N.J.: Revell, 1999).

33. Barbara Jurgensen, *The Lord is My Shepherd, But . . .* (Grand Rapids, Mich.: Zondervan, 1969), 63–66.

34. Dietrich Bonhoeffer, *The Cost of Discipleship* (New York: Macmillan, 1949), 73.

# Index